The Business-Minded
Chief Information
Security Officer

The Business-Minded Chief Information Security Officer

How to Organize, Evangelize, and Operate an Enterprise-wide IT Risk Management Program

Bryan C. Kissinger

The Business-Minded Chief Information Security Officer: How to Organize, Evangelize, and Operate an Enterprise-wide IT Risk Management Program

First published in 2020 by
Business Expert Press, LLC
222 East 46th Street, New York, NY 10017
www.businessexpertpress.com

ISBN-13: 978-1-63742-381-3
ISBN-13: 978-1-95152-751-8 (e-book)

Business Expert Press Business Law and Corporate Risk Management Collection

Collection ISSN: 2333-6722 (print)
Collection ISSN: 2333-6730 (electronic)

Cover and interior design by Exeter Premedia Services Private Ltd., Chennai, India

First edition: 2020

10 9 8 7 6 5 4 3 2 1

Abstract

Information technology (IT) risk and information security management are top of mind for corporate boards and senior business leaders. Continued intensity of cyber terrorism attacks, regulatory and compliance requirements, and customer privacy concerns are driving the need for a business-minded chief information security officer (CISO) to lead organizational efforts to protect critical infrastructure and sensitive data.

While most CISOs report administratively to the chief information officer (CIO), there is a growing realization that this key leadership role requires an individual with both strong technical experience *and* business acumen. A CISO must be able to both develop a practical program aligned with overall business goals and objectives and evangelize this plan with key stakeholders across the organization. The modern CISO cannot sit in a bunker somewhere in the IT operations center and expect to achieve buy-in and support for the activities required to operate a program.

This book describes the thought process and specific activities a leader should consider as they interview for the IT risk/information security leader role, what they should do within their first 90 days, and how to organize, evangelize, and operate the program once they are into the job. It provides practical, tested strategies for designing your program and guidance to help you be successful long term. It is chock full of examples, case studies, and diagrams right out of real corporate information security programs. The *Business-Minded Chief Information Security Officer* is a handbook for success as you begin this important position within any company.

Keywords

information security; cyber security; information risk; CISO; chief information security officer; business-minded; IT; maturity

Contents

Preface

What Does "Business-Minded" Mean?

You might find it an odd title for a book or a bit of an oxymoron to say business-minded chief information security officer (CISO). The truth is IT risk and information security professionals have hidden behind their Certified Information Systems Security Professional (CISSP) certifications and technical jargon for far too long. I recently came across a quote but do not recall who said it. It read, "You can't just rearchitect IT; you have to rearchitect the business." I found this statement impactful and applicable to this publication because many IT professionals think the world revolves around them.

I believe the gap between information security program funding and support has been largely created by information security professionals failing to convey their needs and goals in business terms that senior organizational leaders can understand. Simply put, the business-minded CISO thinks the way the chief executive officer (CEO), chief financial officer (CFO), and board members think; that is, how best can company resources be invested to further the mission, vision, and values of the organization itself?

This concise book will take you through the process of becoming and operating like a business-minded CISO so you can achieve your organizational goals and objectives with the full support of your senior management team and oversight bodies. Let's start with investigating the job prospect.

Acknowledgments

You can't write a book like this without the knowledge and experience gained from coworkers, friends, and family. I credit a lot of this book's content to working with so many bright and dedicated information security professionals. Like many roles in information technology, their efforts are oftentimes unknown and take place behind the scenes. While there are many colleagues to acknowledge, there are a few who have had a particularly meaningful impact on my career. Thank you, Chris Convey, Linda Hill, Ken Lawonn, Mike Corey, Rick Judy, Dick Daniels, Mike Pearl, my parents, and all my friends and colleagues at Trace3.

I want to especially acknowledge and thank my wife, best friend, and security professional in her own right, Teresa McMeans, whose support, coaching, and editing of this book are appreciated beyond words. Without her encouragement, this book would not have been possible.

CHAPTER 1

Before You Take the Job

You're likely reading this book because you are either interested in becoming a CISO/IT Risk Leader, you have accepted a job offer in this role, or you are trying to figure how to do the job now that you are in the role. Regardless of the reason, this book will help you.

There are several key criteria you should evaluate as you enter this level of a role and leadership position within any organization.

Understand the Industry/Company with Whom You Are Interviewing

The CISO/IT Risk Management leader role can vary greatly depending on the industry and specific company in which you are looking to work. Historically, the financial services and retail industries have had the most mature security and IT risk functions. The digitization and consumerization of financial, credit card, and banking data has forced those industries to invest heavily in people, processes, and technology whereas other industries are now playing catch up.

In an interview, you will likely be asked what your industry and market is facing in terms of specific risk, threat vectors, and how your competitors are addressing them, and you have to address these questions if you are new to the role as well. Even as a seasoned CISO, your governing board and other C-level executives will want to understand, on an ongoing basis, how your industry and company compares to others. Certain industries—the health care industry for example—truly value prior experience with IT risk and security leadership roles with other health care organizations. The culture of most health care organizations differs from other industries in that patient care and system functionality and interoperability trump security almost always. That doesn't mean you can't implement a secure environment; it merely means that as the IT risk and security leader, you will need to be cognizant of this philosophy when answering interview questions or later building the program. There are many useful references for learning the trends in IT risk and security for various industries. Gartner, Inc. ("Gartner") and others publish annual reports on leading trends by industry and technology. For example, increasing mobile and consumerization of data is a major trend in the health care industry that is dramatically impacting the delivery and access of information systems.

Prior to interviewing for any position, make sure you thoroughly research the company online. A company's website is usually a great source of demographic information, information about key leaders and the governing body, and the mission and vision strategy. You will also want to know the local market and national competitors/comparable organizations. If interviewing at a large retailer, you will want to demonstrate that you understand how other large retailers think about risk and security and whether they have had any notable public issues worth mentioning. During one CISO job interview, I was asked how the health care industry differed from other industries and what my philosophy was on the security-versus-functionality argument. This is a question for which you want to have a ready answer; otherwise, you will appear to be inexperienced and lacking strategic vision. For example, I was asked, "How do you adjust your approach to securing clinical environments when access and functionality are the most critical facets of technology support?" to which I replied,

> Making systems more secure doesn't have to necessarily make them harder to use. In another health care setting, I was able to implement proximity card access badges for clinicians which logged them in and out to their systems automatically depending on their distance from the work station. This actually made their workflow more efficient and achieved the security objectives I was seeking.

Another great source of industry and corporate information is colleagues within your network. Be aggressive about asking acquaintances about the industry you are entering. If you are fortunate enough to know someone at the company where you are interviewing, ask them about the culture, the challenges, and major initiatives being pursued. This research and preparation will set you apart from every other candidate. It also shows your interest and passion for the role.

Because of the title of this book, I would be remiss if I didn't advise you to think like a "business person." Going into the interview or the new role, you should decide which sort of CISO/IT risk management leader you are. In my experience, almost no one is both deeply technical *and* deeply business savvy. Most CISOs identify as being one or the other: either very technical (often the types that lead technical companies or product security groups) or more business leaning where they understand IT and information security relatively well yet have a closer affinity to translating technical concepts for business and operations teams. For the latter, think "business liaison working within IT." Knowing who you are and having a clear identity is important at the outset. You may find during the interview process or in early days on the job that certain stakeholders value one or the other type of CISO/IT risk management leader. Your ability to secure the job and perform successfully will likely be dependent on what sort of CISO/IT risk management leader your organization is looking for and how it aligns with the culture and organizational structure.

Lastly, have a personality, both at your interviews and in your job. I have found success in these roles by having a sense of humor and generally being able to relate to all levels of employees and many functions across the enterprise. No matter how important you think information security and IT risk management is, it is not as top of mind or as critical to the CFO, internal audit, physicians, and frontline staff. Success at getting the job and being successful in the job will be directly related to the relationships you are able to build and sustain (more on that later). Don't be that nerdy IT person; it's not the 1970s anymore. Showing up with a pocket protector and slide rule will not get you the job. Be a business-minded CISO.

Establish there Is Support for the Program: Governance Structure

You control your interview preparation, industry and company research efforts, and philosophy/personality. You do *not* control—at least at the outset of taking on this role—the level of support and governance structure in place for your IT risk and information security program. There is nothing wrong in asking your prospective boss—or the peers you are interviewing with—about the reputation of the existing team and whether the CIO, CFO, CEO, and governing body values and supports this work. For example, will you have a seat at IT leadership meetings? Will you be able to brief the governing body and related subcommittees directly on risks and program strategy? Are key business unit leaders supportive of this function?

Asking these questions informs your prospective boss and peers that you expect to have a high-level audience for your program. Many "CISOs" (in quotes because often they aren't formally designated as such) have experienced less than successful outcomes because they did not have the appropriate level of visibility in the organization. There is no question that in today's business environment, cybersecurity and IT risk topics are top of mind for corporate boards and C-level leaders. If you will be buffered by another leader, or you get the impression that support for the role and function is not strong, you may want to give this opportunity a lot of thought. It's not impossible to succeed in such an environment, but you will need to spend a lot of your early days building business cases (I'll show you how later in this book) and evangelizing your program.

Figure 1.1 shows a sample governance structure often seen in successful IT risk and information security functions.

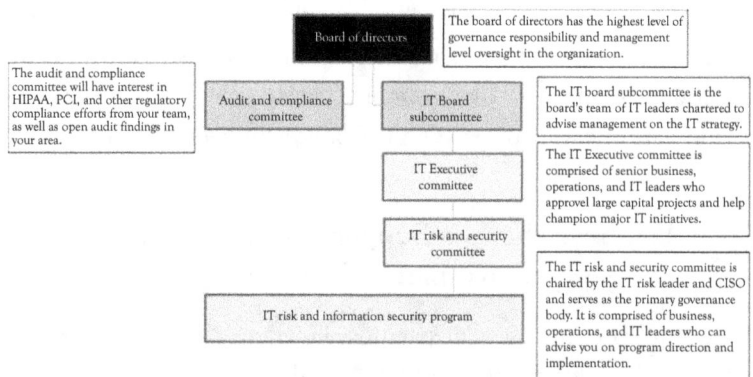

Figure 1.1 Sample IT and information security governance structure

Your prospective or current organization may have a different governance structure, but you should ask during your interview to see what yours looks like and if there will be visibility to these senior leaders and advisors. Value these relationships as you will often find they bring you fresh ideas and provide support for your efforts across the enterprise management team.

Look at the Organizational Chart: Who You Report to and Who Reports to You

I am always surprised to hear leaders who interview for new jobs or take new roles without understanding their position in the organization, who their peers are, and who reports to them. You should absolutely ask your prospective boss for their organizational chart, including the spot you are interviewing to fill. Understanding whether you will be on equal footing with similarly situated peers is critical to deciding whether you will be set up for success or doomed from the beginning.

As important as the governance structure you are inheriting are your peer relationships and the team you will lead. These need to be carefully considered and should be architected in a way that you can successfully carry out your program strategy. Many CISOs have trouble promoting their program because they do not have the appropriate reporting relationships in place. Likewise, if you have a limited team, inexperienced team, or no team, your ability to make rapid progress in your new role could be hampered.

A sample IT risk and information security organizational chart is illustrated in Figure 1.2. Note: This is a traditional model where IT risk

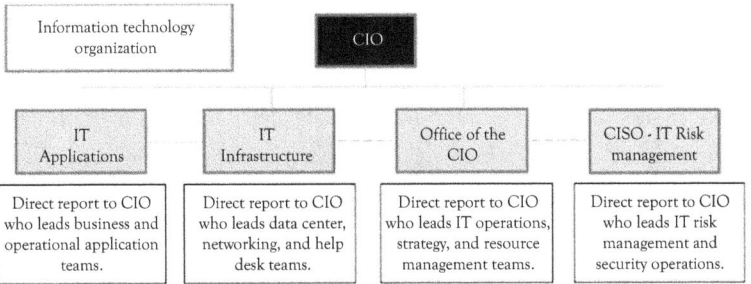

Figure 1.2 Sample IT organizational structure

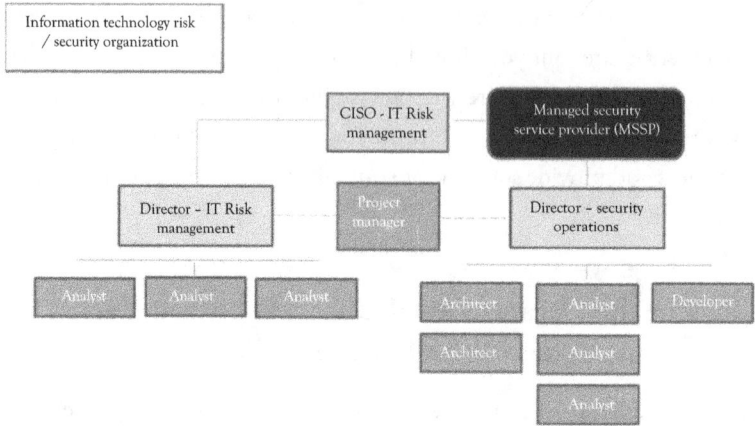

Figure 1.3 Sample IT risk and information security organizational structure

and CISO report to the CIO within the IT department. As it is a recent trend, you may also see CISOs reporting directly to the CEO, CFO, or Chief Risk Officer as this separates them from potential conflicts of interest when needing to exert influence within the IT department. No model is correct or incorrect; the right model depends on corporate culture and where best you can deliver your program most effectively.

The exact titles and number of roles is not overly important in your review of the organizational chart, but you should feel comfortable that the appropriate number of resources are in place or committed to be in place for a successful program. The chart in Figure 1.3 is similar to the one used at a large health care company for their IT risk and security operations team.

Note the presence of a managed security service provider (MSSP). These providers are often providing tier-one support to the security operations team by handling basic alerts and outputs from your log aggregation or security incident and event management (SIEM) solution. The provider sifts through the thousands of daily alerts and notifies your team to investigate and/or remediate only the most important issues. This function frees up your full-time staff to focus on the design of correlation rules, security architecture, and investigation of validated threats. Another key benefit to an MSSP arrangement is that many smaller organizations do not run security operations around the clock. If you have a smaller shop or are coming into a situation where you won't have the staff to provide this coverage, you will want to explore the opportunity to partner with an MSSP to gain this coverage so you may focus your more expensive full-time-equivalent employees (FTEs) on more strategic activities. You most likely don't want to pay and try and retain security professionals in your organization who simply stare at a screen all day.

In one of my previous CISO interviews, my prospective leader provided me with the organizational chart for all of IT. Page Two was my prospective organization. I was able to ask some questions about the job titles, roles of the team in relation to other IT teams, and ascertain my role's relationship to other direct reports. You will want to make sure your role is properly positioned with peers and that you have enough staff (or will be allowed to hire/contract) for the right mix to be successful. During another interview, I was able to have the job title elevated a level up and negotiate two additional requisitions for my team prior to accepting the offer. Remember, you get what you negotiate—not what you deserve!

Agree on Existing/Future Budget Commitments

Now that you have reviewed the organizational chart and the company/industry you are looking to join or lead, you should ascertain the existing budget as well as future budget commitments. There is a direct correlation

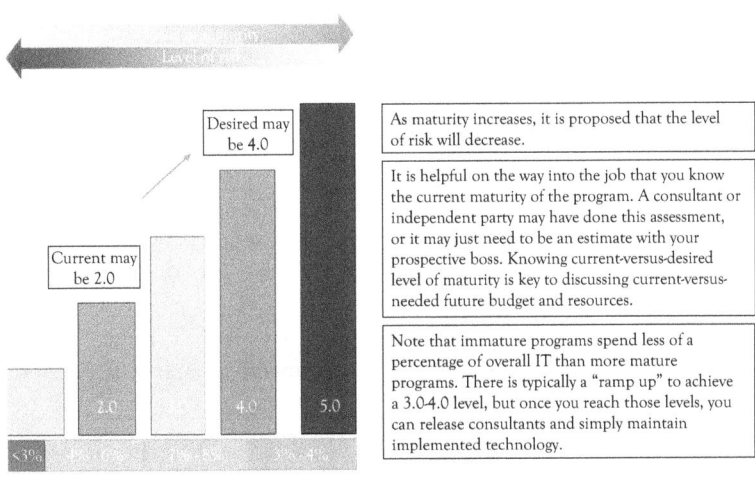

Industry Information Security Budget (% of IT Budget)

Figure 1.4 Example of program maturity measurement

between the funds set aside for your program and your program's ability to implement all your great ideas.

I have argued for years that spend on IT risk and information security efforts directly impacts the maturity of the program and level of risk reduction you are able to achieve. The Capability Maturity Model® is a useful tool to document and communicate existing and desired program maturity. Similarly, the percentage of program spend as a compared to the overall IT budget is a widely used benchmark for program maturity.

Figure 1.4 is an example of how mobile phone signal bars can be used to illustrate a current-versus-desired state of maturity. A simple graphic is also included to illustrate the risk reduction expected by evolution in program maturity.

Explanations for each of the maturity level are detailed below for your reference.

Level 1.0	*Initial:* IT risk and security processes are ad hoc, disconnected, and disorganized. A few individual advocates exist, but no formal program is in place. There is limited but increasing awareness and acceptance across the organization of the need for a formal program.
Level 2.0	*Developing:* A vision is outlined and management buy-in is secured for a formal program. Requirements are assessed, responsibilities are assigned, and the implementation plan is initiated. Gaps are identified. Communication and education programs are rolled out across the organization.
Level 3.0	*Defined:* Goals, practices, and performance metrics are fully defined. Processes are standardized, integrated, documented, and implemented. A formal governance and compliance model is in place.
Level 4.0	*Managed:* The program is part of the culture and is an integral, inseparable component of ongoing operations and decision making. Performance is highly predictable.
Level 5.0	*Optimizing:* Processes are fully mature. Investments and decisions are linked. Feedback from stakeholders is used to adjust and continually improve processes as people, technology, and business requirements change and opportunities arise.

It goes without saying that if you feel uncomfortable with the level of financial commitment to the program, or the current-versus-desired level of maturity, you may want to pass on this role. There are some organizations and senior leaders who believe hiring a CISO or IT risk management leader alone is enough to solve their problems. Unless you are a very hands-on leader, highly technical, and at a small, simply organized company, this is not a single-person role.

It is far better to ask these questions on the way in to a job so you know what to expect; otherwise, you may jump at a job opportunity only to realize you are set up for failure due to lack of funding or desire to mature the program. Several months into your new role, no one will care that budget wasn't adequately considered—senior leaders and governing bodies will just expect results. Get the commitment on the way in and you will be thankful you did. Think like a business person and negotiate the role. You will set the tone for your entire tenure in this position.

Summary Points

1. Before you take a new CISO or IT risk management leader role, do the research. Understanding the industry and organization you are looking to join can be a significant factor in whether you want the job and/or you are able to secure the job. Use the Internet, social media, friends, family, and colleagues to garner information on your prospective organization.
2. Ask to understand the governance structure and organizational charts for the program. If there is little support from senior leadership or you are not positioned well with peers, you will have a difficult time implementing your game plan.
3. Make sure there is an adequate current budget as well as a commitment to fund the program at an appropriate level going forward. Use maturity and spend benchmarks to understand and communicate current-versus-future program goals.
4. Think like a business person. There may be IT risk management and CISO roles (particularly in product companies) that want a highly technical—dare I say, nerd—but in any situation, your ability to understand the business and relate your skillset to address business goals will set you apart.

CHAPTER 2

First 90 Days on the Job

Establish Trust and Credibility with Peers and Key Stakeholders

Whether you were promoted into the CISO or IT risk management leader role or you are new to the organization in this position, establishing trust and credibility with your peers and key stakeholders is critical.

Your first act after the new-hire orientation should be to identify your peers and key stakeholders and meet with them individually. Some key stakeholders may not warrant an ongoing meeting schedule (like the CEO or governing body members), but your IT peers and key stakeholders at your level (likely the compliance or internal audit leaders) should be on your calendar for monthly one-on-one meetings. You can keep these to 30-minute meetings and, of course, cancel if there is nothing new to discuss, but these connection points create a steady cadence and audience for you to learn about your program's effectiveness. It also affords you the opportunity to float ideas and hear what they are working on and how your team might support their efforts.

You may find you can create synergies and goodwill with mutual stakeholders if you team up with these peers to achieve similar goals and objectives. As an example, in one position, I recognized that our vice president of internal audit conducted an annual series of interviews with senior leaders across the organization. The purpose of the meetings was to gather input for the following year's audit and assessment plan. Knowing that I needed to gather information on IT risk for my first annual enterprise IT risk assessment, I asked if I could team up with her, attend these meetings, and ask a few high-level IT risk questions. I sweetened the pot by volunteering to modernize her interview questionnaire by making it much more visually appealing and easier to follow. She took me up on this offer and we "killed two birds with one stone." Leaders we interviewed were thrilled that we condensed two meetings into one, that we both brought new information to the meeting, and that we had streamlined the interview materials. What did I get in return? I got my high-level IT risk assessment questions answered, I accumulated many ideas to help enable the business from my team's efforts, and last but certainly not least, I got to meet a lot of leaders I normally wouldn't meet outside of such an exercise.

Aside from the partnership benefits you will receive, it will be vital for you to consistently demonstrate to your peers and key stakeholders that you are addressing (or at least thinking about) their IT risk and security concerns. This is how you earn trust and credibility.

This next part applies to everything you do in life but is certainly relevant in your new leadership role. *Do what you say you are going to, do it timely, and do it well?* Nothing, again, nothing diminishes your credibility faster than failing to deliver on your commitments. It will be important to jump on that low-hanging fruit, fix people's pain points, and deliver on your promises early. Remember the phrase, "First impressions are lasting impressions?" So true in this arena. What you do in your first 90 days to pull thorns out of people's sides, show you care about using your program to help them be successful, and be a good team mate will set the tone for your career in the role.

Do something "excellent" for your peers and key stakeholders. I wish to relate another anecdote: I was meeting with a senior business leader during my first 90 days on the job as CISO and he expressed extreme pain and frustration with our faxing policy. It became evident that someone in IT had told him (years prior, of course) that faxing sensitive information was the only acceptable means of transmission for hard copy forms. This was contrary to the desired mode of transmission, which was scanning and e-mailing or using an electronic faxing application. The leader further explained that he had multiple employees spending all their time using the antiquated fax process and that morale and productivity were low. I volunteered to investigate the decision and see if I could "pull out that thorn." It took me less than a week to review the decision history, collaborate with our compliance and IT operations departments, and return with a solution that completely met their needs. I made a friend and earned trust and credibility with this business unit with little effort on my part.

Investments of your time to build these relationships, personally, will pay dividends beyond what you can comprehend in the short term. Earning trust and credibility with peers and key stakeholders is crucial in your first 90 days. Do it!

Prior Assessment/Audit Report Review

If you are very lucky, you may come into a role where a newly delivered program assessment was provided to management. One of my recent CISO roles, and my director's role, was created based on management responding to a third-party IT risk and security program assessment. The assessment specifically identified a lack of seasoned program leadership and a current program maturity level of 1.8 out of 5.

In addition to the leadership gap, the report identified several areas of immaturity and risk. The program was lacking formal risk assessment capability, incident response process and documentation, training and awareness coverage, and certain technical safeguards that peers had already implemented. The assessment was conducted by a reputable, large consulting firm, so I took the results at face value.

To complement the assessment report I inherited, I asked the internal audit department for a summary of findings from the past two years of IT audits. This objective window into the performance of the IT organization and security team was valuable in understanding what gaps existed from their perspective and where we stood in terms of management action plans to address the issues. For example, these reports confirmed for me what I had already suspected: inventory and management of clinical/biomedical devices were very immature, and management was struggling with a solution to mitigate the risk this situation presented. Good to know information when you are new in the role! You may find, as I did, that you are inheriting several audit findings with near-term expectations on remediation—also good information to know early in your role. You will want to make friends with your internal audit team and view them as a strategic partner to advance your program's goals. To do this, make sure you put addressing their audit findings at the top of your list. You won't want to appear on a list to senior management or to the governing body as the leader who is delinquent on their management action plan.

Conduct/Refresh Program Gap Analysis

You have come into your new role and have reviewed the existing program assessment (if there is one). You have also perused a summary of internal audit findings related to IT and/or security. You now have a historical perspective on what others think about your program. Within your first 90 days, you should either conduct your own assessment (if one doesn't exist) or refresh the assessment based on your knowledge and experience.

Conducting or refreshing the program gap analysis achieves multiple objectives. First, it lets your boss and peers know you are knowledgeable in your field and are looking to bring your own insights into the areas where the program can improve. Second, it is a valuable mechanism to learn about the existing IT and security architecture, organization, strengths, and weaknesses. Lastly, your assessment—combined with previous assessments and audits—will form the basis for your program business case and three-year plan.

If you have never conducted your own program gap assessment, do not fear! This chapter contains all the relevant information that you can use to evaluate, along with a few examples and templates you can use to communicate your results. Once you have done a few of these, you will become a pro and have more than enough artifacts to conduct these efficiently. Warning: Don't rush to hire a consultancy to do this work on your behalf. Part of the reason *you* are conducting the assessment is to learn the environment yourself and demonstrate *you* have opinions on what areas to focus. Your peers do not want to engage with your consultants; they want to engage with you directly. Recall the previous advice on building and maintaining peer relationships. This activity is part of that process.

All that said, if you have assumed the leadership of a team, you should certainly engage them in the process as they likely have much of the historical information you need. For example, has someone tried a solution in the past and failed? Why? This intellectual property is something you should tap into early in the assessment. You will look foolish if you propose a risk mitigation strategy in your plan only to learn it knowingly isn't feasible based on your unique IT architecture.

Let's get started. How do you organize your assessment? I like to keep things simple, as any good business-minded CISO would. Organize into

People, *Process*, and *Technology* components. These are categories to which the CIO and other senior leaders can relate and easily understand.

People

No matter how much technology advances or how many security tools you have, you will need highly skilled and intelligent people to help you manage your program. In fact, the continued acquisition of technology often begets the need for more people to manage it. You will want to carefully balance your recommendations around hiring, cosourcing, outsourcing, and automation.

I have been a witness to IT colleagues who have made the critical mistake of creating an organizational chart, hiring lots of people, and then trying to figure out what those people are going to do or how to keep them busy. This practice is not good for them and makes you look like an "empire builder." The business-minded CISO thinks like a businessperson by making decisions about spending money and hiring employees as if it were his or her own money. Hire when a need absolutely exists and only when it is more cost-effective to bring on an employee versus a consultant or managed service provider. You will score significant points with your boss and other senior leaders by achieving more with less and running a lean shop than touting how large your organization has become and how many employees report to you.

The following explains how to conduct the *People* assessment.

Since organizations are all somewhat unique in terms of size, industry, culture, and focus of the IT risk and information security program, you will need to understand what is expected from your team. Quick example: In some organizations, the IT risk and information security department handles all aspects of the program, which means they perform security operations functions (provisioning, deprovisioning of access), incident management and response, IT risk assessments, training and awareness, firewall and endpoint management, and so on. Conversely, some programs have a narrower focus with other IT operational teams managing network and security help desk functions. You need to ascertain what role your team plays in all of this today and what the expectations of your team are going forward. It could be that other teams have been covering for

Process	Sub-Process	Service Name / Data Source	Operations Action	Frequency	Paged	Service Owner	Operator Title
Security Incident and Response	IPS Alerts	Endpoint Agent	Operator will respond to critical alerts during working hours	Daily	Yes	Joe Analyst	Sr. Analyst

Figure 2.1 Sample service offering inventory

yours and want to hand things back. In other instances, you may determine that you are covering a function that does not belong in your group.

You should inventory the current and desired functions in a service catalog. I have used Microsoft Excel or SharePoint in the past, but any tool that will help you list and document these will work. Beside each function or offering, you should list who on your existing team is responsible, how many hours a week it requires, intervals, and other vital statistics. Figure 2.1 is a screenshot of an example from SharePoint.

Note that the service owner in this example is blocked to protect their privacy, but all other information is actual databased on an intrusion detection system (IDS) alert function performed by a security operations team. The hours per week metric is listed as 10.0 under the effort column. This data point is the most crucial to capture because once you have your current and desired service catalog completed, you can perform a simple division equation to quantitatively and objectively communicate your staffing needs. Here's how it works.

Let's say for simplicity that your team currently has 10 functions or services that are performed on behalf of the organization.

Function/Service		Weekly Effort
1.	IDS alert monitoring	20 hours
2.	Incident management	10 hours
3.	Enterprise risk assessment	10 hours
4.	Help desk tickets	14 hours
5.	Policy review/revision	1 hour
6.	Audit responses/remediation	10 hours
7.	Training and awareness	20 hours
8.	Vulnerability scanning	15 hours
9.	IT risk advisory/consultation	30 hours
10.	Data loss prevention	10 hours
Total Hours Weekly		140 hours

Equation: 140 hours/40 hours in a work week = 3.5 FTEs

This is a model for a small company with a simple IT environment. Certainly, a large bank or health care organization would have many more functions, hours of effort, and FTEs associated with the program.

Now let's say you currently have two FTEs on your team. You are currently operating at a 1.5 FTE deficit and unless you have a 0.5 person laying around, you have a 2.0 FTE deficit. In this situation, you could make the argument that you either need to hire two FTEs or find a service provider to take on some of the functions/services you are expected to perform. This is the beginning of your business case analysis.

That was a current state analysis. What if during your function/service catalog inventory effort you are asked or expected to take on five additional functions? You are asked to add:

Function/Service	Weekly Effort
Business continuity planning	20 hours
Identity and access management	80 hours
Regulatory reporting	4 hours
Human resources investigations	10 hours
IT compliance	120 hours
These additional functions add:	234 hours

Your future state equation now looks like:

140 current + 234 future = 374 weekly hours/40 hours a week = 9.35 FTEs

This is where the fun starts! You will be happy to take on these additional responsibilities, but you are not going to be able to handle it with your existing two FTEs. When you speak with your boss and governing body, this analysis (along with alternatives) will be your vehicle for a meaningful discussion. You may ask and receive the additional FTEs, especially if your team is newly formed or being formed around you. Alternatively, you may ask your senior stakeholders what functions or services you should remove to meet your FTE future state allotment. Lastly, you may be able to outsource some of these functions and achieve them without having to hire additional employees.

I caution you not take on a significant amount of additional functions or responsibilities on behalf of the organization if you are not provided the people to achieve the desired outcomes. This is not the time to try and be a hero. You should be courageous enough to convey the need to your leadership and/or work with them to arrive at a compromise where you have the right number of resources to be successful.

The numerical equation above is just part of the *People* evaluation.

Often in management you are fortunate to work with what I describe as "athletes." Athletes are employees that can do almost anything, have a passion for learning, require almost no oversight, are self-motivated, and overall make your life easy. Within your first week of taking on the IT risk leader or CISO role, you should meet individually with your team members and begin to ascertain whether you have any athletes. Athletes can sometimes do the work of two or three FTEs. Conversely, poorly performing employees sometimes do the work of 0.25 employees. You need to evaluate your existing team to finalize the number of team members you will ultimately need to deliver on program expectations.

Obviously, you would like to have a small team of athletes and no poor performers, but you will rarely be that fortunate. You should attempt to "coach up" your poor performers and support and encourage your athletes. Ultimately, you may have to make do with the staff you inherit, but hire slowly, one at a time, and build an athletic team around you.

Lastly, you may have the right number and skill sets on the team you have, but are they in the right reporting structure, have the right job titles, being compensated appropriately? This is your chance to make a big difference to your team internally—and on your way into the job. In one new CISO role, I immediately restructured the reporting relationships to divide the team among my directors and I so that we could give more personal attention to each of the team members and focus them on specific functions. I also reclassified several of their roles and was successful in getting them pay raises. While no one outside of our team knew or cared about these changes, it meant a lot to our team and I was able to earn some quick respect points with them.

Process

The best way to build and maintain a sustainable IT risk and information security program is to ensure you have documented and practiced processes. According to *Merriam-Webster's Online Dictionary*, a process is defined as "a series of actions or operations conducing to an end." In the IT risk and information security world, having standardized, documented, trained, and practiced processes is critical to managing a mature program that can respond as expected in a crisis and produce a desired result.

A process is something that someone on your team or some piece of technology is operating or executing for you to achieve a desired outcome. "Security alert and event management" is a process on most security operations teams. This process is usually managed by people on your team using various bits of technology. What you will likely find in your first 90 days is that this process, and many others, may be happening but won't be clearly documented and your staff may or may not be trained appropriately.

Below is a sample list of processes you should assess.

- Enterprise IT risk assessment and management
- Security alert and event monitoring
- Security incident response and recovery
- Threat and vulnerability management
- Identity and access management
- Data loss prevention
- IT vendor risk assessment
- Training and awareness
- Policy and procedure development/revision
- IT risk and security governance

The following is a brief description of each of these processes, as well as the key assessment points associated with each.

Enterprise IT Risk Assessment and Management

Whether you know it or admit it, you are in the risk management business. The most important and meaningful process you need to assess is how you conduct IT risk assessments and manage IT risk on an ongoing basis. The risk assessment should gather inputs from various sources across the enterprise. The *National Institute of Standards and Technology (NIST) Special Publication 800-30* is a useful guide for crafting your risk assessment approach and assuring others you didn't just make up an approach on your own. The guide can be accessed online at http://nvlpubs.nist.gov/nistpubs/Legacy/SP/nistspecialpublication800-30r1.pdf

Whether or not you use NIST as a reference, you should tailor your approach to fit your industry and organization. In the health care industry, the *Health Insurance Portability and Accountability Act of 1996* (HIPAA) Security Rule requires periodic risk assessments of the protected health information (PHI) environment. For many in this industry, HIPAA regulatory and meaningful use attestation requirements must be baked into the risk assessment and risk management efforts of the team.

The risk assessment report should drive the risk management activities of the organization. With financial, technological, and human resources limited in most organizations, you will have to design and operate your program based on risk. Most organizations have enough critical or high-risk findings to keep them busy, so using the risk assessment process to identify these is paramount. To manage IT risks on an ongoing basis, many are turning to electronic governance, risk, and compliance (eGRC) platforms to assist in the tracking and monitoring of risks in a register-type format.

Key assessment points:

- Do you conduct periodic IT risk assessments?
- Do the risk assessment inputs include incident reports, interviews, internal audit reports, vulnerability scan results, and other inputs that provide a lens into IT risks enterprise wide?
- Does your risk assessment framework consider specific regulatory or business process requirements (e.g., Payment Card Industry Data Security Standard (PCI DSS))?
- Do the risks identified have meaningful risk mitigation plans associated?
- Do the critical risks identified have owners who are accountable for the risk mitigation plans?
- Do you have an eGRC platform to help you automate the IT risk management functions?

Security Alert and Event Monitoring

One of the key functions of the security operations team is designing alert features in your environment and monitoring for security events that trigger them. Security tools should be configured on endpoints, internal network, and perimeter devices to alert when certain actions occur or thresholds are met. For example, if you only operate in the United States, you could have an alert or rule configured to send an e-mail to your analysts when someone logs into your network from a foreign country. Your security alert and event monitoring process should establish the design of these alerts and correlation rules, establish a method for ranking their severity and priority, and identify the follow-up actions analysts need to take as a result.

Key assessment points:

- Do you have an existing and documented security alert and event monitoring process?
- Does it include roles, responsibilities, process flows, and desired outcomes?
- Has the process been tested in a table-top exercise or is it routinely practiced during security operations team meetings?
- Is the process documentation revised based on the test results and any technology changes?
- If this function/process is outsourced to a third party, how are you kept informed on their ability to monitor for your alerts and events?

Security Incident Response and Recovery

The security incident response and recovery process is subsequent to the process described above. It is considered a separate process because often alerts and events do not rise to the level of requiring the invocation of a response and recovery action. If an event alert does present a significant concern, this security incident response and recovery process will be the most important one you manage. This process identifies and documents the specific roles and actions that security operations and other

IT operational teams should take during this critical time. Unlike an IT event where the goal is to restore systems as quickly as possible from an outage, a security incident response and recovery process may dictate that you preserve certain system memory (forensic images), disconnect systems, or disconnect from the Internet completely. The design of your response and recovery program should include taking advantage of your network segmentation strategy (if you have one), quarantining certain hosts or subnets, preserving forensic data and images, and restoring from backup media.

Response may include the invocation of an emergency response retainer, engagement with law enforcement, or participation by key vendors. Recovery may require the participation of key vendors or consultants to rebuild damaged systems and/or repair critical data sets.

Key assessment points:

- Do you have an existing and documented security incident response and recovery process?
- Does it include roles, responsibilities, process flows, and desired outcomes?
- Has the process been tested as a table-top exercise or is it routinely practiced during security operations team meetings (in coordination with the security alert and event monitoring process)?
- Is the process documentation revised based on test results, real events, and any technology changes?
- If this function/process is outsourced to a third party, how are you kept informed about their ability to respond and recover your critical systems and data stores?

Threat and Vulnerability Management

Threat and vulnerability management are extremely important functions your team should be performing every day and in real time. Understanding the likely threat vectors for attack in your industry and your company will help you design the right proactive and detective safeguards. You cannot protect everything all the time, so having a sound process to identify and evaluate threats—as well as conduct regular vulnerability management activities—is critical to a risk-based program.

The Federal Bureau of Investigation (FBI), the Department of Justice (DOJ), and National Information Sharing and Analysis Centers (ISACs) are among the organizations that are partnering with private companies to share threat intelligence. In addition to these organizations, many next-generation security tools come with Open Threat Exchange (OTX) or fee-based threat intelligence capabilities. In some cases, leveraging an MSSP makes a lot of sense considering having threat intelligence or malicious software ("malware") researchers on staff is not feasible for many organizations. Ask yourself: Will your team really know about the next zero-day attack from Eastern Europe before a large MSSP who specializes in this work around the clock?

Vulnerability management can be achieved by ensuring you have a process in place to regularly scan your network and devices—both as they are provisioned to the environment and once attached. There are many tools and service providers in the market for vulnerability scanning—just ensure the reports they produce are actionable and risk-based. Simply having vulnerability scan results with 10,000 lines of vulnerabilities is neither meaningful nor actionable.

Key assessment points:

- Are the likely threat vectors for your industry and company known?
- How are indicators of compromise (IOCs) identified in your network?
- Are security events logged and monitored? Are events to be logged clearly identified?
- How are threats identified, triaged, and mitigated?
- How are patches managed? Do you have specific thresholds for critical versus important security patches?
- What steps are taken to protect systems against malware? Are the scope of systems and scope of malware clearly defined and updated?

Identity and Access Management

The identity and access management (IAM) process at your company is an important component to the overall protection of your network infrastructure and sensitive data. This is especially true for privileged or "super users" in your environment. The IAM process governs how access is provisioned, modified, terminated, and escalated.

A good process balances the need for security with the ease of use and functionality available to your user community. Depending on your industry, you may have greater success with tighter controls in this space, or you may have to live with leaning more toward the "ease of use" side of the continuum. For example, in the health care industry, adding clicks or steps to the login process can be difficult to implement in a clinical setting. Health care professionals are pressed for time and focused on providing care and charting. Asking them to use military-grade logins will not make you popular with this group of stakeholders. You could potentially be a hero, though, by designing and implementing secure single sign on (SSO), proximity badge sign on/off, or biometric sign on. These solutions are not only secure but make logging on and off easier.

Privileged users, such as database administrators, have access to large caches of data and typically move this data around for testing, reporting, and other valid business reasons. Strictly managing their identity and access rights is a must if you are to protect your company's most valuable information assets. Network administrators usually try and have shared credentials to administer network appliances, firewalls, and so on. *Don't allow this practice.* Look to implement a privileged access solution or password vault solution to manage, monitor, and audit these accounts.

Key assessment points:

- Do you have a policy and procedure for granting, modifying, and revoking access for applications and supporting infrastructure for all users in your environment?
- Does the policy and procedure identify privileged accounts and special management practices for them?
- Does your IAM strategy consider SSO or federated access models for various stakeholder groups? For example, you may

want customers or frontline staff to have streamlined sign on and application-to-application pass through of credentials to provide for a more efficient user experience.

Data Loss Prevention

Data loss prevention (DLP) is simply the practice of using people, processes, and technology to prevent sensitive data from being accessed internally or externally by unauthorized parties. If you are fortunate to have a data classification scheme, it is simple to apply DLP tools based on classification. For example, what your organization classifies as "secret" information may be blocked completely from transmission outside of the corporate network. DLP tools can scan endpoint devices, e-mail messages, and other repositories—as well as web traffic—and take actions based on predefined rule sets.

If you do not have an enterprise wide data classification scheme (many do not), one of your key assessment activities should be to understand what types of data you have in your environment, and where your most sensitive information is stored/transmitted. Certain business units may have a legitimate business reason to share sensitive information with others in the organization or external partners who are part of your operations. Without a clear data classification strategy, you will need to identify these business units and work with their management to apply DLP controls so that a balance between functionality and security can be achieved.

Key assessment points:

- Does your organization have a data classification scheme?
- Do you have a data protection policy that considers data at rest, data in transit, and data on endpoint?
- Do you have a DLP strategy, including the use of DLP tools that proactively act on policy violations?
- Are you addressing all sensitive data storage and transmission media in your organization (e.g., personal cloud storage uploads, use of personal e-mail and webmail accounts, unsecure electronic data interchange (EDI) such as file transfer protocols (FTPs), etc.)?

IT Vendor Risk Assessment

IT vendors have, over time, come to represent a large proportion of organizational vendors overall. Very few business projects are devoid of any IT impact. Everything runs on information systems, and IT vendors are important partners in achieving organizational goals and objectives.

Partnering with IT vendors can be both a strategic advantage and an administrative nightmare. You need them to deliver IT functions, but they introduce risk and complexity that you would not normally have in working with a solely in-house IT team. To determine the level of risk an IT vendor is introducing, and to determine whether the benefit outweighs the risk, you should have a standard IT vendor risk assessment process. This process should be initiated early in the procurement process so that vendor selections can be guided by the results of your assessment. Often, I have seen the IT vendor risk assessment conducted after the vendor has been selected and contracted, or even a week before a deliverable from them is due. This late engagement renders the risk assessment process moot.

You should make sure you have a standard assessment criteria checklist that evaluates the vendor's compatibility with your IT environment, their information security safeguards and controls, their service level agreements (SLAs), regulatory and compliance adherence, and other factors to help facilitate a smooth integration into your environment. Make sure the IT risk assessment facts and decisions are well documented so they can be referenced later.

Key assessment points:

- Are existing IT vendors inventoried? Are current and legal department-approved contracts in place with existing IT vendors (e.g., SLAs, Business Associate Agreements (BAAs), Non-Disclosure Agreements (NDAs))?
- Are new IT vendors subject to a review process by various teams within IT?
- Is there a recurring, standing technology review committee that follows a standard checklist or procedure for risk assessing new IT vendors?

- Are enterprise wide procurement functions educated on the technology review committee process and required to consider the committee's review prior to a purchase decision?

Training and Awareness

No matter how much process improvement you make or fancy technology you implement, maintaining a secure and relatively low-risk environment requires assistance from your people and user community. Phishing e-mails are a perfect example. All the web filters in the world will not prevent some malicious e-mails from reaching your user community. One phishing campaign my team initiated to gather the company's baseline statistics resulted in a 36 percent click rate on simulated phishing e-mails that were sent.

The only way to reduce this surprising fail rate is to increase training and awareness activities on the subject. Beyond phishing, there are many other topics for which technology users need regular training and awareness. Think about physical security, protection of mobile devices, safe password management practices, and acceptable use of social media. You must strike a balance between information risk and security training and awareness activities. If you are too much in the user community, they begin to tune out. Not enough, and they forget. I have always found a quarterly training schedule to be about the right balance.

The first activity of your training and awareness program should be to assess where you have the highest risks or concerns and build out a training and awareness campaign schedule to address those areas first. Be creative. I have been using 30-and 60-second videos to deliver key messages, interesting posters in break rooms and common areas, quizzes and blogs on our intranet site, and so on. If you build interesting content and make it available to everyone on a useful intranet page, you will see success in the campaigns you produce.

Key assessment points:

- Do you have a training and awareness program beyond annual mandatory compliance training?

- Have you assessed your organization's weakest security knowledge areas and built a campaign schedule to address them?
- Are you creating interesting content tailored to your various organizational audiences? Training for bank tellers might be very different than training for banking application developers.
- Do you have an intranet site where content, news, and other information security learning material can be accessed by the workforce?
- Do you have metrics defined to evaluate the effectiveness of your training and awareness program?

Policy and Procedure Development and Maintenance

While not the most exciting security topic to discuss, policies and procedures are the foundation on which we communicate expectations of behavior to users. Most information security policies and procedures are rooted either in legal or regulatory requirements, industry standards, or leading practices. It is almost always the first place an assessment or audit of your program will focus, followed by how well your organization complies with them.

Policies should be short, easy to understand, and reviewed regularly. No one will read or try and understand a 70-page information security policy. My favorite approach for policies and procedures is to create short, specific documents on granular topics such as remote access, acceptable use of IT systems, and so on. If you can keep the policies to just a few pages, people can access and read those they have questions about quickly rather than paging through a novel.

Make sure your policies are on your intranet site where they can be easily located and reviewed. I cannot express how many times I have consulted at a company that thinks the world of their information security policies and procedures; yet when I inquire of everyday users, they have neither seen the policies nor do they know where to turn if they have a question.

Key assessment points:

- Do you have information security policies and procedures?

- When is the last time they were revised? Policies that are more than one to two years old are likely outdated or have sections that are no longer applicable due to technology and business changes.
- Are your policy and procedure documents short and easy to comprehend by the average end user?
- Are your policies and procedures stored on your intranet where users can easily access them?

IT Risk and Security Governance

While not a process per se, you should evaluate how IT risk and security decisions are discussed and supported across the organization. I'm not talking about day-to-day decision making, but the big decisions that impact broad sets of stakeholders. For example, if you are terminating access to personal cloud storage at your company, you better have had a broad discussion with stakeholders to determine both the impact and acceptance of such a decision.

As discussed in the opening chapter, I find having a dedicated committee for IT risk and information security governance to be extremely valuable. Membership should represent a broad cross-section of your organization and be made up of experienced leaders who can truly speak on behalf of their business units. This governance team will provide you with invaluable feedback on any significant IT risk and security proposal, as well as be your advocate/evangelist for the work out in the field. Treat these folks right and they will support you; leave them in the dark, and they will fight you every step of the way.

Key assessment points:

- Do you have at least one governance team that provides feedback and direction for your program?
- Do they meet frequently enough to support you in driving key initiatives?
- Is the membership composed of the right breadth and leadership level to help you make key decisions quickly?

- What is your value proposition to them? Do you keep them informed on key plans, proposals, and performance metrics?

Technology

IT risk management and information security technologies are a critical component of your program. That said, don't fall for allure of "it does everything" or "a single pane of glass" sales pitches that the thousands of vendors in this space are spouting. Undoubtedly, the next-generation technology available to us as practitioners is helping to automate parts of IT risk management and security operations, but you must guard against purchasing "shelf ware" or multiple point solutions from which you will only utilize partial functionality.

One approach to assessing your technology capabilities is to use the *Lockheed Martin Cyber Kill Chain® Framework* as a mapping tool, which can be found online at https://lockheedmartin.com/en-us/capabilities/cyber/cyber-kill-chain.html

The Cyber Kill Chain framework is part of the Intelligence Driven Defense® model for the identification and prevention of cyber intrusions activity. The model identifies what the adversaries must complete in order to achieve their objective. Stopping adversaries at any stage breaks the chain of attack, ideally at the earliest stage possible. Adversaries must completely progress through all phases for success; this puts the odds in our favor as we only need to block them at any given one for success.

The kill chain model is designed in seven steps:

- Defender's goal: understand the aggressor's actions.
- Understanding is intelligence.
- Intruder succeeds if, and only if, they can proceed through steps 1–6 and reach the final stage of the Cyber Kill Chain.

Figure 2.2 shows an example of how to graphically represent current technology capabilities to desired technology capabilities. Note that the mapping is vendor agnostic; the focus is on what you want the technology to be able to do for you. I have found this method of visually depicting

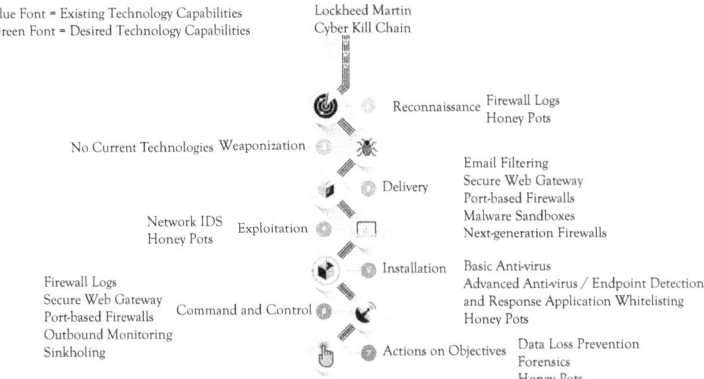

Figure 2.2 Sample current technology capabilities versus desired technology capabilities

Source: https://lockheedmartin.com/en-us/capabilities/cyber/cyber-kill-chain.html

current versus desired technology capability to be impactful. You could also use a separate map to illustrate when you would be able to implement this technology—more on this later when we discuss your business case and three-year plan.

Building this map will take a little time during your assessment. Likely, your team will not even own or operate some of these technologies, so you will need to get out and speak with the network, infrastructure, application, and web services teams to determine where these technology capabilities exist. That said, try not to get caught up in who owns what. As the new IT risk management or CISO leader, it is far more important to build relationships with these teams than to attempt a "land grab" in your early days in the role. Over time, it may make sense for some of these technologies to be managed by your team, but it is far safer to let the existing teams continue managing them while you are assessing your own program and team's skills.

There is a compelling argument that it is far better to be a consumer of data from these various sources (into your log aggregator or SIEM solution) than to administer and operate each of these solutions yourself. In other words, don't look a gift horse in the mouth. If someone or some other group is willing to administer these for you, you may benefit from that structure by being able to deploy your team to more strategic, risk management, and security operations-type functions.

Architecture

As part of your technology assessment, you should spend some time with your network and/or security architects. Certain security technology solutions may have been purchased and installed due to the unique way your network is architected. Similarly, your unique network architecture may limit your ability to implement certain security technologies. You should understand these earlier decisions and future limitations as part of your assessment and technology mapping.

As an example, retail organizations typically have a significantly decentralized network architecture. They may have thousands of point-of-sale locations that require network architecture and security technologies to similarly operate while decentralized. On the other side of the coin, a single hospital provider organization may have one Internet connection and a data center in the basement. Understanding the existing architecture and architecture plans for the next few years will play a major role in your decisions around security technology.

Lastly, you may be inheriting technology that you wish you weren't. I once started a role where the infrastructure team entered into a five-year contract with an endpoint security vendor that I was forced to live with for four and a half years. The cost and effort to "rip and replace" this solution was certainly not worth getting my preferred technology in place, but this earlier decision severely limited the security technology solution I could attempt on endpoint. I shifted to network-and perimeter-based security technology evaluations where I have the flexibility to rationalize and replace technologies that had expiring licenses or where existing solutions did not exist.

Pricing, Vendor Evaluations, and Proof of Concepts

You are the most popular person in your company now! You will be invited to as many happy hours, fancy dinners, and sporting events as you can possibly handle. Security vendors have grown exponentially over the past five years. If you recall what the vendor exhibition hall looked like at the RSA conference back then compared to now, you know what I mean. While I don't have the statistics to prove it, it certainly feels like most startups are in the security technology space or have a significant security component embedded as a selling feature.

First and foremost, realize you are in a strong bargaining position. Security technologies—particularly startup vendors—have tremendous flexibility in how much they can charge for their licenses, appliances, and/or services. Be a strong negotiator. Certainly, don't pay list price. If you work for a nonprofit or academic institution, ask for reduced pricing based on your tax status. If your company is willing to let the vendor use you as a reference client publicly or use your logo on their website or marketing slicks, often the vendor will cut you a break on pricing as well. Every time—yes, every time—I have rejected a vendor's first quote for their technology, they have chased me down with a significantly lower price. You must drive hard bargains since every dollar you spend with a vendor is budget you won't have for process improvement or human resources.

Vendor evaluations are always an interesting exercise. Your first question to a security tool vendor should be, "What existing security capabilities do you replace, combine, or enhance?" If they can't give you a convincing answer, you might choose to move on from them quickly. Most vendors can perform similar security functions in their space, but are they better at it than their competitors? This is where proof of concepts (POCs) come in.

A POC is a great way to understand how well the security technology meshes with your infrastructure, as well as how well it performs against peers. If you are evaluating malware sandboxing solutions, try to plug them in at the same time and see how they perform concurrently. I did this exact POC and found that one technology vendor's product significantly outperformed the other. POCs should be free from the vendor and last at least 30 days. If you can convince the vendor to let you POC their solution for 60 or 90 days, even better. Before beginning your POCs, make sure you establish what the purpose of the POC is, what the expected outcomes are, and the success criterion for those solutions. It will be helpful in building your business case—which will be covered in the next chapter—to have these report cards when you are budgeting and planning the implementation of these solutions.

I have encountered multiple scenarios where the technology looked great but didn't work in our environment. Just as many times, it worked great, solved a problem, but I could not afford it. You can cut to the chase very quickly with vendors if you start with the following premise. I say to every vendor who is pitching me a new product (feel free to steal these lines), "I'm the easiest person in the world to sell to. If we need your product, if it works in our environment, and we can afford it, I'll buy it. I control the first two and you control the last one."

Lastly, you may find that your architecture, budget, staffing level and experience, or other factors lend themselves to considering an MSSP. MSSPs are in this business full time and provide SIEM, network threat hunting, malware sandboxing, and practically every other service or capability you are looking to buy and maintain yourself. Do this assessment first, determine whether your ability and cost to manage these technologies is lower, and then call in MSSPs for discussions. Once you have this assessment complete, you will know what you may want their services for and can then request bids to fill the gaps you can't fill yourself.

Key assessment points:

- Do you have an enterprise wide inventory of security technologies and capabilities?
- What does your existing architecture support in terms of enhanced security tools?
- Have you evaluated the existing technology contracts and commitments to understand where you are in the existing refresh lifecycle?
- Are you able to map out existing versus desired technology capabilities using a tool like the Lockheed Martin Cyber Security Kill Chain?
- Are you capable of conducting POCs of concurrent technologies to compare performance?
- Do you have an existing MSSP relationship or are you able to articulate the potential use cases for entering one?

Maturity Versus Risk Measurements

Assessing a program is typically a highly subjective exercise. It is difficult to quantify—on say, a Likert scale—how experienced your people are or how effective your processes or technology are at mitigating risk. That said, assigning a numerical value for both maturity and risk in each of your program functions will help establish a baseline from which you can measure progress over time.

Thus far, we have discussed key points for assessing your people, process, and technology components, but a more detailed approach will be outlined—along with an example output—in the next chapter as part of developing your business case and three-year plan. For now, let's discuss sources of technology risk and how technology risk is created.

Sources of risk can broadly be attributed to two categories: "insiders" and "outsiders." Insider risk is often a result of well-intentioned staff who sometimes expose sensitive information when corresponding with outside parties. It could also result from uninformed or unaware employees engaging in risky behavior intentionally or unintentionally. Outsider risk is what most security teams focus on and includes malicious outsiders who are looking to steal sensitive information to use for themselves or to sell in the ever-growing information black market. The most common outsiders include nation-state sponsored, organized crime, and hacktivists. Despite the majority of focus and security spend on addressing outsider risk sources, over 40 percent of data breaches are the result of insider actions (half intentional, half accidental).[1]

What is technology risk? Here is the simple definition: A risk exists when a vulnerability can be exploited by a threat source.

As an example, Figure 2.3 is a graphical representation of risk creation in the retail industry.

There are a plethora of frameworks to reference when ranking risk in your technology environment, but which one to pick is not nearly as important as applying that choice to all your risk assessment activities in

---

[1] Seals, T. 2015. "Insider Threats Responsible for 43% of Data Breaches." *Infosecurity Magazine.* http://infosecurity-magazine.com/news/insider-threats-reponsible-for-43/

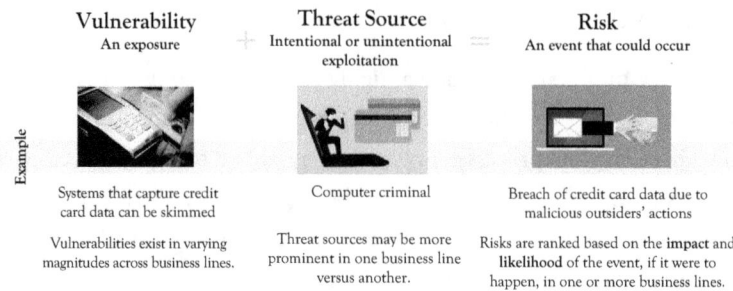

Vulnerability	Threat Source	Risk
An exposure	Intentional or unintentional exploitation	An event that could occur

Systems that capture credit card data can be skimmed	Computer criminal	Breach of credit card data due to malicious outsiders' actions
Vulnerabilities exist in varying magnitudes across business lines.	Threat sources may be more prominent in one business line versus another.	Risks are ranked based on the **impact** and **likelihood** of the event, if it were to happen, in one or more business lines.

Figure 2.3 Graphical representation of risk creation in the health care industry

Source: Icons from https://pixabay.com/

order to have apples-to-apples comparisons over time. If you use a five-by-five risk ranking scale one year, and then switch to a three-by-three scale the following year, you will spend more time converting risk rankings than addressing the risk.

Figure 2.4 a simple risk ranking criteria map I have used over the years.

Using this approach, a maximum score on the likelihood and impact scale would yield a score of 25 [5 (Likelihood) x 5 (Impact)]. In Figure 2.4, this would result in a critical risk and be represented in the far upper right corner. Of course, ranking the likelihood and impact on this one-to-five scale is subjective, but you can develop and align organizationally on what *very low* means as opposed to *critical*. Maturity ratings were similarly discussed on a one-to-five scale using the Capability Maturity Model® as a

		Risk severity				
Likelihood	Almost certain	Very Low	Low	Medium	Critical	Critical
	Likely	Very Low	Low	Medium	High	Critical
	Possible	Very Low	Low	Medium	Medium	High
	Unlikely	Very Low	Low	Low	Low	Medium
	Rare	Very Low	Very Low	Very Low	Low	Low
		Very Low	Low	Medium	High	Critical
				Impact		

Very Low = 1, Low = 2, Medium = 3, High = 4, Critical = 5

Figure 2.4 Sample risk ranking criteria map

Program component		Maturity[1]	Prior period	Risk[2]
Threat and vulnerability management	• Intrusion detection / prevention solutions • Vulnerability scanning / remediation • Advanced threat / anomalous behavior monitoring			High
Incident and event response	• Security event playbook • Response drills • SIEM monitoring capability			Medium
Training and awareness	• Security awareness and education • Tailored communications • Stakeholder engagement			Medium
Security architecture	• Network and system architecture design • Asset management • Security configuration management		No Change	Medium
Privacy and data protection	• Information classification / requirements • Encryption / Data Loss Prevention (DLP) • Data malware protection		No Change	Medium
Identity and access management	• Authentication and authorization • Remote and mobile access • User role management and review		No Change	Medium
Regulatory support and policy compliance	• Security policy/procedures management • Legal / regulatory compliance / audit support		No Change	low
IT risk management	• Security program governance / organization • Risk assessment / review • Performance measurement / reporting		No Change	low

1 Based on the industry standard Capability Maturity Model (CMM) definitions for 5 levels of Maturity

2 Calculation based on threat risk plus level of vulnerability/capability

Figure 2.5 Program maturity-versus-risk analysis

Source: Icons from https://thenounproject.com/

reference. Using this maturity-versus-risk comparison is helpful in prioritizing resources in the lowest maturity/highest risk areas of your program.

An example of this analysis is represented in Figure 2.5.

With a similar analysis completed at your organization, you will have the foundation communication vehicle for people, process, and technology needs discussions with your CIO and other senior leaders. Remember to think like a businessperson. Keep it simple and use the examples in this chapter as references for developing your own assessment that other business leaders can understand.

Summary Points

1. Your first 90 days on the job are critical to your long-term success as the new CISO or IT risk management leader. You must build relationships and earn credibility early to pave a path of success for your program initiatives.

2. Take advantage of prior assessments, audits, or reviews of the IT risk management and information security program as it accomplishes two goals. First, it accelerates your knowledge of the environment

by leveraging work others have already completed. Second, it shows that you are considerate of your peers' and stakeholders' time *and* that you will not visit with them to ask the same question an auditor asked two months ago.

3. Conduct your own assessment using simple, easy-to-understand criteria like people, processes, and technology, evaluated on risk and maturity scales. If you present a practical, reasonable assessment of your program in business terms, the likelihood of you successfully selling your business case and three-year plan (discussed in Chapter 3) will greatly improve.

CHAPTER 3

Organize Your Program

Functions of an IT Risk Management Program

There are many authoritative sources that can guide you in the formation of your key program functions. Over the years, I have melded my personal experience as a consultant and seeing what works at companies across a variety of industries using noteworthy frameworks such as NIST and the International Organization for Standardization (ISO).

Figure 3.1 an example of a program I have implemented and its mapping to the *NIST Cybersecurity Framework*, which can be accessed online at https://nist.gov/cyberframework

You can certainly call your key program components whatever you would like but I prefer these terms as most business stakeholders can relate easier than some "technobabble," which requires explaining. Each of these program components is described below:

IT Risk Management

IT risk management is the overarching program component where your annual and ad hoc risk assessments are conducted, where your technology review committee is facilitated, and where your governance and risk

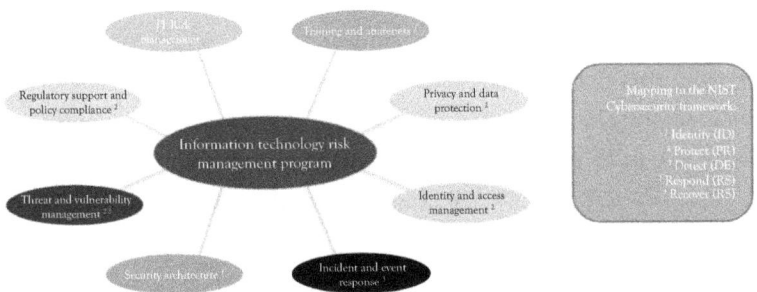

Figure 3.1 IT risk management program mapped to the NIST Cybersecurity Framework

compliance (eGRC) platform tracks and reports IT risks. This component sets the tone for your entire program. Your ability to effectively identify and communicate IT risks in business terms will determine the look of your business case, your approved funding levels, and ultimately, what risk mitigation activities you will engage your team in throughout the year.

As you design your IT risk management program, you should consider a couple of key factors. First, consider the scope. Most organizations are complex, and their organizational structures are often built around different legal entities, affiliations, and/or laws, regulations, and other requirements. Hopefully the scope of your IT risk management function covers the entire entity so that top-level decisions on risk treatment apply universally; however, you may find that different parts of your organization are simply unable to be in scope due to the legal or geographic organizational structure. That's fine, just make sure you caveat your risk management work so that it only applies to the entities in scope.

Second, it is critical that you achieve buy-in on roles and responsibilities in your IT risk management program. Internal to your team, you will want to assign someone responsible for maintaining a risk register or risk inventory. If you have an eGRC platform, most of them come embedded with this capability. If you don't have an eGRC platform, using a spreadsheet or other lower technology solution will work as well. The purpose of the risk register is to document, track, remind, and report on active IT risks you have identified during your risk assessment process.

Now that you have a risk register and someone on your team managing it for you, you will need to assign primary risk owners to those risks. The role of the primary risk owner is to have a single, accountable party ensuring the risk mitigation plan is carried out. Note that the primary risk owner may need a lot of support from others in IT and the organization to successfully address the risk, but they are the person who is going to drive the team's remediation efforts.

The IT risk leader and/or CISO plays an important role as well. Not only are you the leader of this program, but you should expect to be the primary risk owner for many risks that fall under information security categories. Another role you will play is the escalation point for risk treatment decisions. You will likely need to be the mediator between other primary risk owners and operational teams who are being asked to affect some change to address a risk. It can be challenging to get all parties agreed on a course of action, but that's where you as the business-minded CISO intercede and bring a practical resolution that is acceptable to everyone.

Governance teams play an important role as well. If a risk treatment decision or proposed course of action will impact large parts of the organization, you will want to elevate the risk and proposed solution(s) to your committee for input and consensus. As mentioned earlier in this book, these governance teams can be a strong vehicle for change if you engage them appropriately.

With the scope and roles and responsibilities defined, you should now draft a risk management plan that articulates your vision, your IT risk management lifecycle, your IT risk-scoring methodology, and your IT risk mitigation planning and treatment decision-making approaches. This plan is the artifact you can socialize with key stakeholders, auditors, and others as needed to gain support for your program as well as agreement on methodology.

Training and Awareness

Next-generation technology continues to advance IT risk and information security leaders' ability to safeguard their environments. That said, most experts agree—and the data supports—significant breaches and other cyber security vulnerabilities are the result of employee/user error. Consider the rise in the success rate of phishing and spear-phishing attacks at delivering malicious software and stealing legitimate credentials. Most e-mail and Internet filtering technologies are still not 100 percent successful at identifying and blocking these malicious e-mails from reaching internal recipients.

The most effective way to supplement your technical controls and program processes is to implement a robust training and awareness program aimed at your highest risk audiences. In fact, at every company I have been in an IT risk/information security leadership role, I have insisted on having a full-time employee solely focused on training and awareness, communications, and stakeholder engagement. Here are the facets of a successful training and awareness program:

- Needs assessment
- Campaign schedule
- Content development and delivery
- Communications and stakeholder engagement
- Effectiveness measurement

Needs Assessment

How do you know *who* to train, *what* to train them on, and *how* the training is to be delivered if you don't conduct a needs assessment? Needs assessments can be conducted in a variety of fashions, from automated, fun gaming platforms to low-tech interviews and reviews of audit/assessment results. I have utilized a cloud-based workforce security awareness assessment tool that allowed me to evaluate thousands of employees' awareness of basic information security knowledge with little more than a click of a few buttons. The assessment used interactive games to test the recipient's understanding and report a score back to the tool. I was then able to look at aggregated and disaggregated reports to determine where our common weak spots were, what the weakest areas of the organization were, and what priority of training content I should develop and deliver.

While this is a fancy approach, I have also had success with simply interviewing various leaders and employees across the organization to assess their level of knowledge and where they believed they needed more training. Audit or assessment reports, as well as actual incident reports, can also provide a wealth of information of areas to focus. If you are seeing many incidents in your environment due to employees posting sensitive information to social media accounts for example, you should certainly consider a social media "campaign" (explained in the next section) in your plan.

Think of your approach in terms of the following:

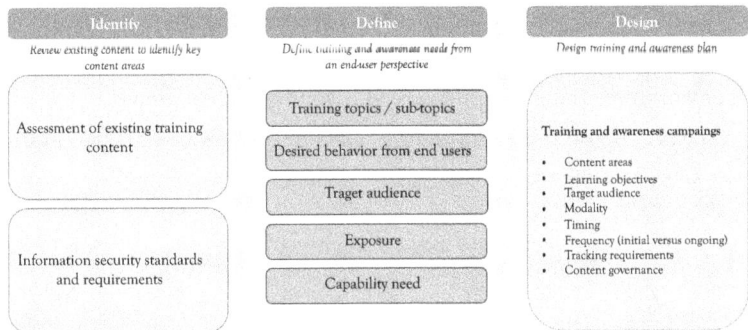

Figure 3.2 Sample approach to developing a training and awareness campaign

Campaign Schedule

Now that you know where you highest gaps in security awareness exist, you can begin to formulate a rolling calendar of training including delivery methods. Creating a campaign schedule is a balancing act. Most organizations have an annual compliance training period where employees drudgingly complete web-based training modules to fulfill state and federal regulatory training requirements. While the training process can be tedious for employees, once per year is simply not enough training in IT risk and information security topics to truly be effective.

The frequency of training I have found to be the right balance is quarterly. In addition to the annual compliance training period, I plan four additional campaigns each year for a three-year period. I use the needs assessment results to target the highest risk areas first and then make sure I have coverage over all significant information risk areas over the three-year plan.

This training schedule should outline both the topics to be covered each quarter as well as the target audience(s) for each. For example, you may decide to conduct fake e-mail phishing campaigns to the entire workforce each quarter (based on risk) but have the third quarter be targeted IT developer training in secure web coding. Again, caution must be taken not to overburden the workforce or any one group of employees with too much training. You can achieve the opposite of the intended effect by having employees become numb to information security topics. To that effect, a wise approach is to partner with your compliance, legal, and human resources departments to understand their training schedules, thereby ensuring you aren't competing with an annual employee survey or other workforce training initiatives with your quarterly launch.

Here is an example of a training schedule over a one-year period for three specific audiences (Figure 3.3):

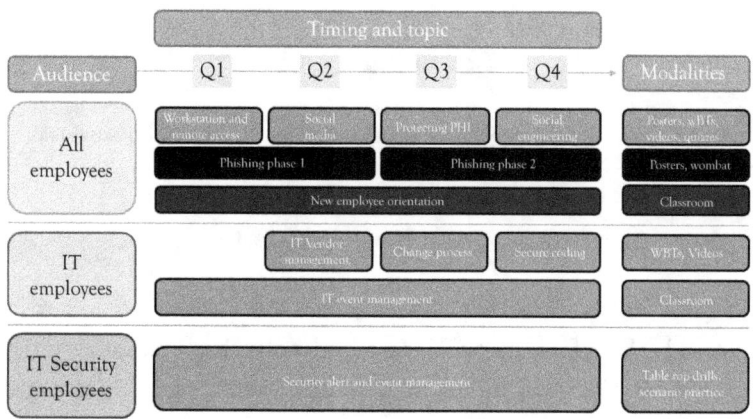

Figure 3.3 Sample training schedule

Content Development and Delivery

You now have the *what* and *who* aspects of the plan figured. Next, we will discuss the *how*. Your content creativity and quality will vastly influence the success of your program since innovative and entertaining content is always more effective for user interest and retention than boring old slide presentations.

Raise your hand if you enjoy sitting in front of your computer for hours, or repeatedly hitting the "next" arrow on slide decks to complete your mandatory compliance training. No hands? I'm not surprised; it is amazing to me that, despite the many options for creative content development and delivery options in the marketplace, these antiquated methods are still the norm.

The most successful content—and some of the least expensive—are developed in short, vignette styles with a catchy theme. Consider this: Would you ever watch a five-minute television commercial? Probably not; but an entertaining, catchy commercial is one people often talk about long after it has aired. You should strive for this level of interest in your campaigns. Just because we are delivering IT risk and information security training doesn't mean it has to be boring and uninspired.

With that said, how best do you develop content that is interesting and quickly digestible, delivered in a way that won't disrupt normal workflow (too much)? As an example, developing and delivering security awareness training content for physicians must be approached very differently from how you would develop and deliver privileged user training to IT staff. Put yourself in the shoes of your target audience and think about how you would react to the content you are deploying. Here are some creative ways to develop and deliver content:

- Use screen savers as opportunities to splash awareness messages.
- Employ "teachable moments"; for example, little flash videos or comic strips that appear for a user after they click on fake phishing e-mails sent from your phishing training platform.
- Posters are an inexpensive way to communicate and remind employees about things they should be thinking about throughout the day. Display catchy posters in break rooms or other employee areas that utilize just a few words to deliver a key message.
- Create and maintain a dynamic intranet site for your program and provide as much content and news as you can there. Drive visitation by putting the intranet site's address in your (and your team's) e-mail signature line and mention it as a one-stop shop for all resources related to your program.
- Use your intranet site to host short quizzes that reward employees with small gifts or program SWAG (Stuff We All Get) if they take the quiz and achieve a minimum score.
- Create leadership forum and staff meeting briefing presentations that you, members of your team, or departmental security evangelists can walk through at regular team meetings, huddles, and new hire orientation. In my opinion, in-person delivery of interesting content, anecdotes, and real-life examples remains the most effective form of raising security awareness.

Security Tips

These tips will keep you safe when working remotely
from the comfort of your office workstation.

DO Flag suspicious emails, even from a known source.		**DON'T** Click on hyperlinks or attached documents in generic emails.
DO Report security incidents timely.		**DON'T** wait to report lost or stolen data and other IT assets.
DO Turn on auto-lock features and screensaver protections.		**DON'T** leave your screen unattended where sensitive data can be viewed.
DO Use complex passwords to protect log-in access.		**DON'T** use the same password across all your applications and systems.
DO Contact the IT help desk if you suspect malicious activity.		**DON'T** Try to address a hacking attempt on your own, IT staff can help.
DO Back up sensitive data and system settings.		**DON'T** Keep sensitive files on your local hard drive – use a back up location.
DO Limit personal use on corporate IT resources.		**DON'T** Use corporate IT assets for non-company business.
DO Be aware of social media policies and be careful about public postings.		**DON'T** Post pictures and information that you do not have permission to do so.

*Source:*Icons from https://pixabay.com/

Be creative. Better yet, have the creative people on your team mockup ideas for you. There are also many training programs available which you can license inexpensively to help your team create fun and informative content. The following graphic is just one good example.

Communications and Stakeholder Engagement

Training and awareness efforts can take many forms. In this chapter, I have discussed traditional activities focused on determining need, developing content, and then delivering that content to the appropriate audiences.

When organizing your training and awareness program, make sure you have someone on your team who is managing your communications and stakeholder engagement plan.

The plan doesn't have to be fancy; I often use a workbook or spreadsheet in order to have sortable views available. You will want to identify your major program stakeholders so that you can document who you should be meeting with, how frequently, and what topics should be/have been discussed. If you haven't yet had a chance to meet a lot of other leaders, start with the organizational chart and list the top leaders of each business unit. Your program will benefit in several ways by being diligent in stakeholder engagement.

- Business and operational leaders will have an opportunity to provide input into IT risk and information security concerns their teams are facing. They are your eyes and ears out in the field.
- These leaders will tell you where they feel they need additional training and awareness efforts for their departments (a key input to the needs assessment).
- You will have the opportunity to promote your team's work and demonstrate value.

Below is a blank example of a stakeholder engagement plan. Tailor the format and information to your needs. You will want to revisit this plan at least monthly to ensure you are engaging with your key stakeholders regularly and that you are following up on actions and feedback you have committed to address. Stakeholder engagement is most effective when you take their input seriously and close the loop in terms of what you and your team have done in response.

IT Risk and Information Security Program
Stakeholder Engagement Plan

Figure 3.4 Sample stakeholder engagement plan

Effectiveness Measurement

Peter F. Drucker, the writer, management consultant, and college professor is credited with the quote, "What's measured improves." Measuring the effectiveness of your training and awareness program is key to be a business-minded CISO. Whether you have a generous budget, a small budget, or no budget for training and awareness efforts, your ability to demonstrate value for your workforce and key stakeholders is critical.

Metrics for effectiveness can sometimes be difficult to design and measure, but here are a few ideas I have used successfully:

- If you are deploying fake phishing e-mail campaigns to raise awareness of this threat, start by baselining your recipient's response rate. As an example, when I launched an internal fake phishing campaign, I didn't alert anyone that it was coming. This is known as a "blind phish." I was alarmed when my organization's click rate (or failure rate) was 36 percent on average. I instantly knew this was a high-risk area for us and that more training and awareness was required. After developing several training and awareness tools, I retested the organization with another blind phishing campaign. The click rate had dropped to under 20 percent, nearly a 50 percent improvement on desired behavior. This metric clearly measured the effectiveness of these phishing campaigns.
- If you are driving traffic to your intranet site as a one-stop set of resources, most sites allow you to count the number of total page visits and unique users. While it doesn't give you a direct effectiveness measure, being able to report that 50 percent of all employees are visiting your site or downloading training material is important for substantiating the efforts put forth to maintain the site.
- Many employees are overwhelmed with corporate surveys. They range from opinion to fact-finding to most anything else you can think of. That said, using a survey or assessment tool to follow-up after a training and awareness campaign can prove valuable in measuring the absorption rate. For example,

if you just completed three months of focus on remote worker safeguards and you send out a quick assessment tool or game, you would hope to see high success rates in respondent answers. If you don't, you may have a gap in your content or delivery mechanism.

Privacy and Data Protection

The privacy and data protection component of your program is mostly concerned with your most sensitive data, such as where it is stored, how it is transmitted, who has access to it, and what happens if it is inappropriately accessed or disclosed. Not only is safeguarding your employee and customer information the right thing to do, many state and federal laws and regulations exist, which penalize organizations for not being diligent in applying appropriate safeguards.

Here are the major subcomponents of privacy and data protection to organize:

- Information classification
- Confidentiality, integrity, and availability requirements
- Cryptography/encryption
- Information handling standards for electronic media

Information Classification

To protect information, you must know where to focus your efforts. Unless you are in a very small company, you will likely find data strewn across the organization in structured (e.g., applications and databases) and unstructured (e.g., file shares and decentralized repositories) sources. To apply protective safeguards most efficiently, consider classifying information by importance to business operations.

An information classification scheme should apply across the organization and consider a number of key factors: take into account of the potential business impact of a loss of confidentiality of information; be used to classify information stored in both electronic and paper form; be applied to information associated with business applications, computer installations, networks, systems under development, and end-user environments; and explain how to resolve conflicting classifications.

Some organizations also consider requirements for integrity (i.e., the need for information to be valid, accurate, and complete) and availability (i.e., the need for information to be accessible when required) when classifying information. Techniques to communicate the classification of information include labeling information, recording details in an inventory, providing awareness training, and incorporating classification details in contracts (or equivalent).

Designing and implementing an enterprise wide information classification scheme can be very challenging. Ownership of information is often a source of contention and without clear ownership of key data sets, often classification schemes break down. I suggest starting small. Pick a pilot department or team and analyze all the data they use and their sources. If you can come up with a classification scheme for one department or team, you can often build on that success and create concentric circles of classification.

Typical classification levels include:

1. Restricted or Secret (top level)
2. Confidential
3. Company-Internal
4. Public- or Company-External (lowest level)

These are just examples. Depending on your industry and organization, you may have information that fits best in one or more classification levels. Once you have information classified into schemes or levels, it is important to label, store, process, and provide access to it appropriately.

Newer versions of business applications and e-mail systems are building into the platform itself the ability to have user-generated labels for e-mails and documents. Once labeled, your DLP system or e-mail security solution can look for these labels and take the appropriate action. For example, if a user labels an e-mail "Confidential" based on the available tags, the e-mail security solution can detect and auto-encrypt the contents for the user before it leaves the network (Figure 3.5). This is a nice,

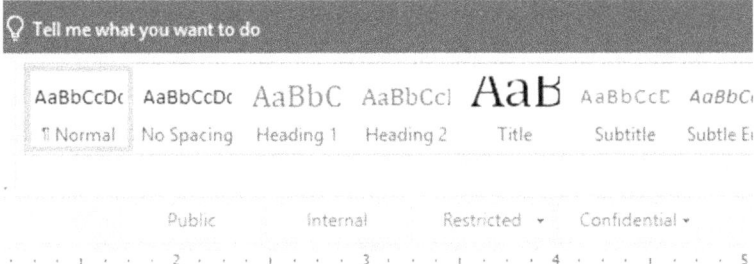

Figure 3.5 Label options embedded into an e-mail application

automated control that helps prevent errors related to having to manually encrypt an e-mail within the user interface.

A risk-based approach suggests that you spend most of your resources securing your top-level classification information, also known as "crown jewels." One strategy companies use to organize their data by importance is network segmentation, a topic to be covered later in the "Security Architecture" section. Whether or not you use segmentation, you should certainly apply most of your risk mitigation approaches and safeguards to the areas where your most sensitive data resides.

Confidentiality, Integrity, and Availability Requirements

"Confidentiality" means keeping information secret or private within a predetermined group. The impact of business information being disclosed to unauthorized individuals would typically be assessed in terms of: potential loss of competitive advantage; potential loss of business; potential damage to customer or shareholder confidence, public image, and reputation; the possibility of incurring additional costs (e.g., through the need to investigate the loss of confidentiality, take remedial action, or to provide compensation); a breach of legal, regulatory, or contractual obligations; a potentially damaging effect on staff morale or motivation; and the potential for fraud.

In the health care industry, a lot of effort and resources are put toward protecting the confidentiality of patient records. In the financial services industry, focus is mainly on protecting demographic and financial information from thieves. Regardless of industry, safeguards should be applied based on your classification scheme (for example, medical information =

restricted), to help prevent unauthorized access, viewing, or use of information outside the intended audience.

"Integrity" means maintaining the completeness, accuracy, and validity of information. The impact of business information being accidentally corrupted or deliberately manipulated would typically be assessed in terms of: potential loss of competitive advantage; the potential for incorrect management decisions to be made; potential loss of business (e.g., losing orders or contracts); potential damage to customer or shareholder confidence, public image, and reputation; the possibility of incurring additional costs (e.g., through the need to investigate integrity problems or to restore the integrity of lost or corrupted data); a breach of legal, regulatory, or contractual obligations; a potentially damaging effect on staff morale or motivation (e.g., if staff cannot rely on information or a particular system); the potential for fraud (e.g., unauthorized diversion of goods or funds); and the potential disruption of business activity.

Many internal controls design efforts, such as Sarbanes–Oxley (SOX) Section 404, are designed and implemented to maintain integrity of data. In the case of SOX, the goal is internal controls for financial reporting. The *Sarbanes–Oxley Act of 2002* was designed to give confidence to investors that financial reporting coming from public companies is accurate and maintains its integrity throughout the financial reporting process. Let's face it, if we are all dependent on information systems to conduct business, operating with inaccurate information or data that has integrity flaws can be catastrophic.

"Availability" means ensuring that information is accessible and usable when required by an organization. The impact of business information being unavailable for any length of time would typically be assessed in terms of: potential loss of competitive advantage; the potential for incorrect management decisions to be made; potential loss of business (e.g., losing orders or contracts); potential damage to customer or shareholder confidence, public image, and reputation; the possibility of incurring additional costs; a breach of legal, regulatory, or contractual obligations; difficulty in recovering from a backlog of processing; a potentially damaging effect on staff morale or motivation; the potential for fraud (e.g., goods or funds being diverted fraudulently); and the potential disruption of business activity.

Having worked at companies across many industries, I can definitively say that operations and business teams care most about availability. It's great to have strong security that protects the confidentiality and integrity of information, but if their computer, application, or favorite system is unavailable, you will hear about it immediately. From an IT risk perspective, preventing down time due to poor change management practices or cybersecurity attacks should be at the top of your program agenda. The recent rash of ransomware attacks on companies has highlighted weaknesses in availability and resiliency of multiple corporate infrastructures. If you cannot operate your business effectively without your IT systems, you should make every effort to design and implement redundancy, segmentation, and backup strategies to combat potential availability issues.

Cryptography/Encryption

Cryptography can be used to protect the confidentiality of sensitive information. Cryptography can also be used to determine whether critical information has been altered by performing hash functions. Yet another function of cryptography is to verify the identity of the originator of information (e.g., e-mail sender). The identity of the originator of critical information would typically be confirmed using a cryptographic digital signature (nonrepudiation). Approved cryptographic algorithms are listed in Figure 3.6.

Effective cryptographic key management typically includes generation of cryptographic keys, secure distribution, storage, recovery, and replacement/update of cryptographic keys; revocation of cryptographic keys (e.g., if a key is compromised, or a key owner changes jobs or leaves the organization); recovery of cryptographic keys that are lost, corrupted, or have expired; backup/archive of cryptographic keys and the maintenance of cryptographic key history; allocation of defined activation/deactivation

Encryption algorithms		
Purpose	Algorithms	Minimum key length (Bits)
Key exchange	RSA Diffie-Hellman	2048
Data in transit	AES	128 and 256
Hash	SHA- 1	N / A
Storage	AES	256

Figure 3.6 Encryption algorithms

dates; restriction of access to cryptographic keys to authorized individuals; and sharing of cryptographic keys (e.g., using split key generation) required for protecting sensitive information and critical systems.

Encryption practices are usually referenced in three modalities: data at rest, data in transit, and data on endpoint. Each of these modalities will be discussed in Chapter 5. For now, as you organize your program, be cognizant of what encryption mechanisms are currently in use, where they are applied, and how they consider your information classification scheme. You may ultimately decide your current cryptographic and encryption strategies are suitable or you might explore additional safeguards based on new technologies joining your environment or even new relationships that create data transmissions outside of your organization.

Information Handling Standards for Electronic Media

Knowing where your most sensitive information resides is critical to protecting it while in use, as well as when you decommission systems. For instance, hard drives get recycled and make their way onto auction sites for sale. Information handling standards are in place to provide prescriptive and mandatory treatment practices for sensitive information and the devices on which they are stored.

Sensitive information held on data storage media can be protected by: erasing the content of reusable storage media when no longer needed; storing data storage media in accordance with manufacturers' recommendations; recording and approving the transfer of files using data storage media; keeping records of data storage media taken outside the environment in which they are normally used; and removing business information from data storage media prior to sending computers off-site for maintenance.

The transfer of sensitive information should involve the use of cryptography to: protect the confidentiality of sensitive information when transferred; determine whether critical information has been altered during transfer; and enable the identity of the originator of critical information to be determined (e.g., using digital signatures to provide nonrepudiation).

Identity and Access Management

Identity and access management (IAM) concerns how you provision, modify, and deprovision access to information and resources in your technology environment. It is important to be able to establish authenticated identity, validate authorization to access certain resources, and manage that access over time. IAM issues continue to be "low-hanging fruit" for auditors and regulators as most organizations still lack proper hygiene when removing stale accounts or managing users as they move between departments.

Technological advances in this space have helped IAM become more secure (e.g., multifactor solutions and cloud-based security brokers) while increasing the speed and ease in which users can authenticate across multiple applications (e.g., SSO solutions). Self-service employee portals can decrease call volume to your IT help desk by providing certain functions, such as password resets, to be handled by the users themselves.

As you are organizing your program, you will want to understand how IAM functions currently operate. For example, some organizations rely heavily on active directory and lightweight directory access protocol (LDAP)-enabled applications to manage access more efficiently across the enterprise. This practice has pros and cons but would be difficult to unwind even if you wanted to make a change philosophically. Hopefully your organization is using some sort of role-based access or digital rights management solution to prevent each user from having a unique access set up. As mentioned earlier in this book, privileged or super users are the most important user groups to have strong controls around. A typical end-user may have some access to sensitive information, but it is typically one record at a time and accessed from an application. Privileged or super users can access data and critical resources in large-scale volumes and accordingly, their account credentials are the most sought after by hackers.

Key facets of the IAM component include:

- Role-based access
- Authentication
- Credential management

- Monitoring
- User account maintenance

Role-Based Access

With role-based access processes, access to different systems is managed according to defined roles tailored to job functions. Role-based access is granted only to individuals who have been approved by an appropriate manager as needing to have specific access to perform their jobs. You should strive to eliminate customized user responsibilities that are specific to one user, and not based on a role. Access roles are rarely modified and, when modified, are only modified by IT and go through a formal change management process.

The concept of "minimum necessary" should always be applied. Minimum necessary means that users are only granted the minimum necessary access to perform their job functions. If a user requires additional access to perform enhanced job functions, the user should be moved into the appropriate role for that function—rather than having additional privileges added to their existing role. "Segregation of duties" considerations should also be evaluated. Segregation of duties relates to ensuring roles are designed and implemented such that a single user's access doesn't afford the opportunity to perform conflicting job functions that could circumvent other controls. A typical example is an accounts payable clerk versus an accounts receivable clerk in an accounting, finance, or procurement department. You would not want the folks who pay vendors to also be the folks who collect payments on behalf of the organization. This seemingly obvious conflict could create a situation where their access allows them to set up vendors (themselves) and make payments to themselves. Key conflicts like these should be documented in a matrix for each application or system so that roles can be designed and users assigned properly.

Authentication

Authentication is the process of determining whether a user attempting to access resources is truly who they say they are. Access controls and password requirements should be enforced across all systems according to a defined authentication policy and are typically operated by automated access control mechanisms to facilitate individual accountability.

When organizing your program, you should gain an understanding of what authentication mechanisms are in place for various technology resources. For example, do you allow single-factor authentication to web resources from outside the corporate network? It is common to allow employees access to certain intranet resources like their human resources or pay data, but it should be allowed cautiously and ideally with multifactor authentication (MFA) mechanisms. Do password requirements contain the length and complexity to ensure they are not easily guessed? Have default and administrative passwords been changed? Is there have a standard user naming convention so that user names are not repeated or recycled when employees move or terminate?

Federated access or access authentication that is streamlined between IT resources is continuing to gain in popularity. In many ways, these next-generation authentication mechanisms have improved security by making logging into systems easier while requiring stronger user input. Biometric, token, and other multifactor approaches are doing more to validate an authentic user while at the same time increasing the efficiency of access to multiple systems in a single session.

Credential Management

Credential management systems store user identities and credentials, including passwords, certificates, and/or keys, which can be accessed for authentication and authorization purposes. Ideally, credential management systems are centralized and leveraged across multiple applications (e.g., single or reduced sign on) to simplify administration and demands on the user (e.g., remembering multiple passwords and user names).

Helping users manage their credentials efficiently and securely supports objectives for safely authenticating them to the resources they need for their jobs. Stolen credentials, especially those of privileged and super users, is a leading cause of data theft and breach. One of the largest and costliest data breaches of all time was the result of a database administrator's credentials being stolen after he clicked on a phishing e-mail link and allowed keystroke-logging technology to be loaded onto his keyboard.

The keystroke logger was able to capture his administrator credentials and those credentials were used to extract large volumes of sensitive information.

As you organize your program, understand how credential management works at your organization. Determine whether there are opportunities to evaluate single/reduced sign on and utilize active directory for LDAP-enabled applications or other technologies to help manage authentication processes.

Monitoring

Managing access and credentials is the front-end to user lifecycle management. Monitoring user authentication and access to highly sensitive information is the daily operational end of IAM. Your team should ensure sensitive access is logged and monitored for appropriateness—most likely utilizing a log aggregation tool or security event and incident management (SEIM) platform.

All design and maintenance of user accounts can be performed perfectly, but people are still the weakest link of the process. Monitoring critical accounts and events can help provide early detection of compromised credentials or unauthorized use of an account. You may want to know when domain administrator accounts are used versus normal user accounts, or whether privileges are escalated at 3 a.m. when you operate a nine-to-five business. Establishing the appropriate level of monitoring and, most importantly, reviewing and acting upon anomalous events, is critical to heading off potential breaches.

User Account Management

The back end of the IAM is maintaining user accounts to ensure you are only authorizing current employees/contractors to organizational IT resources appropriate for their roles. User account management broadly refers to a set of processes and tools to support the creation and maintenance of a digital identity through its entire lifecycle from initial creation, to alterations, to removal (either by deletion or disablement). A typical user management/administration tool will associate a single user identity to one or more accounts and privileges owned by that user.

A couple of common problems typically arise as part of organizing a user account management program. "Accumulation of access" refers to employees who are initially granted access to IT resources based on their first role at the company, but then accumulate additional access as they change roles without ever having the old role access removed. This is an especially challenging problem with employees who are long tenured at an organization and have moved from department to department over the years without a review of their prior role access privileges. Adding to the segregation of duties example described above, imagine an employee who starts with a company in the accounts payable department and does such a great job that she is promoted as a manager. Her accounts payable departmental access is increased to include greater responsibilities and approval authorities commensurate with her new role. A year later, the accounts receivable department lures her over to become the new director of receivables and she is given high-level access to manage vendor accounts, bank accounts, and other resources. Now the new director of receivables can set up vendors and pay vendors—a clear conflict of interest.

Another frequently encountered challenge is stale accounts, both at the application layer and the network layer. Ensuring that management, human resources, and IT coordinate the termination of accounts when employees leave is critical to maintaining accountable access to your IT resources. I have often heard the argument that active directory access or network layer access is disabled so the application layer account is not as important to maintain. One can argue that can be a viable "back stop" control, but I have seen time and time again where application layer credentials were shared, and the application account continues to be used after the employee was terminated.

As you organize your program, examine how user accounts are managed, what systems are in place to automate the process, if possible, and what, if any, issues your organization has had with stale accounts. Often, internal audit or external assessors will choose an application or two to evaluate active accounts against a current employee list. Financial auditors will typically conduct this exercise once a year during their annual audit of company financials. If they find that stale accounts exist during their review, you may have to prove that those accounts have not been used and that you will implement a process or mechanism going forward that will identify and remove these accounts timely.

Incident and Event Response

The core functions of security operations include the incident and event response component. The process of security incident and event response consists of four phases:

1. Initiation/triage
2. Containment
3. Eviction
4. Recovery

In the initiation/triage phase, you will want to document what alerts, incidents, or events trigger your process and what other processes could or should be invoked as a result. A security alert may trigger an escalation to a security event, which in turn should escalate to an IT event. Likewise, an existing IT event may conclude that the event's underlying cause is a security issue, which should invoke this process. Once the security event and response process is invoked, you will need to assess the severity of the event and determine whether assistance is needed from a third party or law enforcement. Often your internal security and IT teams will be able handle the event, but a severe or rapidly spreading complex event may require you to enact your emergency response services contract or engage law enforcement for assistance.

In the containment phase, you must first identify what the indicators of compromise (IOCs) are so that alerts can be set up to detect additional instances occurring in your environment. Once these alerts are set up, you need to identify the infected hosts, compromised accounts, and data. As when you initiated the incident and event response process, you may need to reach out to third parties or law enforcement for assistance in containing the attack. When organizing your program, make sure you have these relationships in place and that your team has mechanisms in place to contain attacks (e.g., network segmentation, draw bridges, etc.).

In the eviction phase, the security operations team should lead the development of an eviction plan with input from other IT departments. Eviction may be completed in several ways including, but not limited to, black holing network ports, physically pulling network cables, developing scripts to disable hosts, and so on. Eviction of convicted hosts and accounts should happen concurrently to ensure that the attackers do not have time to change their attack vectors.

In the recovery phase, the security operations team should assist the IT infrastructure and applications teams with any necessary forensic information to restore to normal operations as quickly as possible. Often the security operations team will recommend patches or architectural changes to stave off future attacks using a similar vector. Make sure, as part of the recovery phase, that you debrief on the root cause(s) for the successful attack and put in place a game plan to prevent a repeat attack as soon as you have recovered. Keep in mind that patches are designed to be temporary fixes and do not necessarily permanently correct the root issue.

Roles and responsibilities need to be clearly defined and practiced as part of the incident and event response process. In real life, this event can be chaotic with well-intentioned employees taking actions that are detrimental to the containment, eviction, and recovery phases. Encourage creative thinking, but make sure your IT team knows what role they play versus the role your security operations team plays. Practice, practice, practice.

Security Architecture

Security architecture is a set of representations (e.g., blueprints, designs, diagrams, tables, models, and specifications) that describe the function, structure, and interrelationship of security components (e.g., security controls, security services, and security products).

The following security architecture facets will be covered in this section:

- Network architecture
- Change management

- Internet usage
- General security controls

Network architecture

Network devices (e.g., routers, hubs, bridges, concentrators, load balancers, switches, and firewalls) should be configured to:

- highlight overload or exception conditions when they occur;
- log security-related events in a form suitable for review, and write them to a separate system;
- copy control information (e.g., logs and tables to aggregators and/or removable media);
- integrate with access control mechanisms in other devices;
- disable source routing (to retain control within the packet-forwarding device); and
- disable services that are not required for the standard operation of the network (e.g., X Windows, Open Windows, RPC, rlogin, rsh, rexec, and NetBIOS).

Network documentation should include network configuration diagrams showing nodes and connections; an inventory of communications equipment, software, and services provided by external parties; and one or more diagrams of in-house cable runs. Network documentation (e.g., diagrams, inventories, and schedules) should be kept up-to-date and readily accessible to authorized individuals. Management should periodically review network documentation, which can be, ideally, generated automatically using software tools.

As you organize your security architecture component, understand what network segmentation practices are in place. Flat networks, or networks that connect freely between resources without consideration of zoning, create vulnerabilities and exposures to the entire network if infected. The use of zones and subzones, either with hardware or software boundaries, can help control traffic as it traverses east–west in your corporate network. For everyday network management, these zone schemes assist

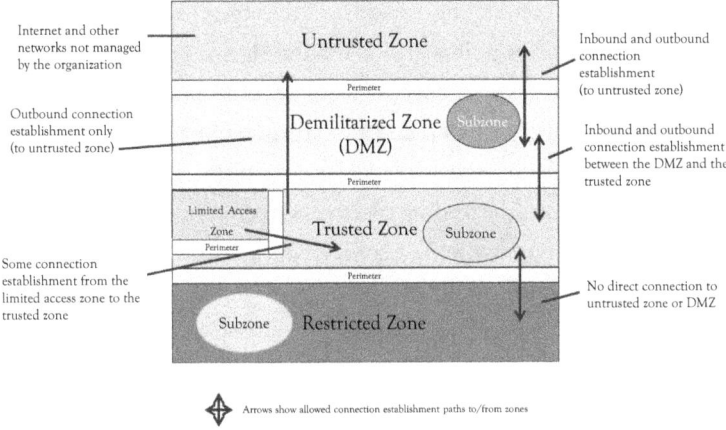

Figure 3.7 Zoning scheme example

administrators in ensuring applications and users operate only within the part of the network needed for their roles. When an attack finds itself on the network, these zone schemes can help contain the attack or malicious software in one area of the network versus being able to traverse freely to all network segments.

Figure 3.7 is an example of a zoning scheme that takes full advantage of multiple zones to control different user groups and resources. In this example, the *Restricted Zone* could be where your most sensitive applications and databases reside and where most of your organization may not need to access for their jobs.

Wireless access should be protected. Authorization of wireless access from approved locations should be enforced by

1. changing security-related default access point settings (e.g., service set identifier (SSID) and the Internet protocol (IP) address);
2. disabling beacons within access points that regularly broadcast the SSID;
3. using IP address filtering to limit access to client computers with authorized IP addresses only; and
4. using media access control (MAC) address filtering to limit access to wireless network interface cards (NIC) with authorized MAC addresses.

Also consider conducting periodic "drive byes" of facilities to test whether wireless access points are emanating signals beyond the walls of the organization. A favorite hack of many security practitioners is to sit in parking lots and try to gain access to corporate networks from a car. If you want to provide access to clients, customers, patients, and other nonemployee visitors, the leading practice is to create a separate and completely segmented guest wireless network they can use but has no ability to connect to corporate resources.

Finally, on the network architecture, is the topic of external connections. External connections might include those used by staff working in remote locations and by authorized third parties. In today's remote workforce and vendor support model, it is not unusual to have hundreds or thousands of virtual private network (VPN) or other remote access connections into the corporate network. Methods of authentication used might include subjecting external users to strong authentication, such as one-time passwords, smartcards, or tokens. You may also provide only a thin client, virtual, or Citrix type of environment to prevent certain functionality to be available to a remote user.

Be sure to have an inventory of remote connections and users and ensure they are all using approved and secure technologies to connect. Stale remote user and vendor accounts represent a significant attack vector as often passwords are shared, and these accounts have historically looser controls as it relates to account management and reviews. Insisting on MFA will provide you a healthy risk mitigation strategy but keeping track of who has tokens and whether they are still needed always presents a challenge for the IT risk and security teams.

Change Management

A key facet of your security architecture program component is your change management process. A change management process would typically address the following:

- Upgrades and modifications to application software, including patches
- Revisions to parameter tables and settings

- Modification of business information (e.g., data tables, files, and databases)
- Changes to user/operating procedures
- Emergency fixes; and
- Changes to computers and networks.

Most organizations operate a change advisory board or similar committee who meets regularly to review proposed changes to the technology environment. This committee should have representation from all parts of the IT department so that changes can be evaluated holistically. For example, a change may have little to no impact on production applications but may require significant input and effort from the endpoint or network team.

As you organize your change management program, ensure there is a periodic review of proposed changes and a process for emergency fixes. The committee should meet frequently enough to implement changes timely and keep the list of changes to a manageable size for members. Large company change management committees will often meet weekly, but smaller companies or companies that make changes infrequently may meet biweekly or monthly.

Internet Usage

Practically every employee has access to the Internet while on the job; therefore, Internet use should be appropriated to restrict access to authorized users and approved functionalities. Users should be warned of the dangers posed by downloading mobile code (e.g., Java applets, MS ActiveX, JavaScript, or VBScript), which have been written deliberately to perform unauthorized functions. They should also be aware of the implications of accepting or rejecting cookies (a small text file containing information that can be used to identify a user returning to a website). Finally, users should be educated on the consequences of opening attachments downloaded from the Internet. Secure web gateway technology can be employed to help protect users and computers from harmful and malicious software coming in through a web browser, but no technology is foolproof. Often website categorization in these tools lag emerging threats. Also, you will likely not be able to use every feature in a secure web gateway tool since certain teams or applications rely on Internet traffic to function.

Your organization should have a clear policy on acceptable Internet usage and the expectations related to responsible use. There is no better way to infiltrate an organization than through the Internet, where an attacker can sit thousands of miles away in a foreign country with little to no risk of ever being identified.

Understand both your primary and secondary organizational connections to the Internet, who and what is authorized to access the Internet, and what technology controls are in place to inspect, filter, and act on suspicious inbound traffic.

General Security Controls

General security controls typically include policy, methods, procedures, and device or programmed mechanisms intended to protect the confidentiality, integrity, or availability of information. There are a multitude of controls frameworks, but I have found the *Center for Internet Security's (CIS) Critical Security Controls* to be a concise and useful guide.

The CIS Critical Security Controls are categorized into 20 sections covering asset management, secure configurations, malware defenses, and data backup and protection, among others. The framework is publicly available for free download at: https://cisecurity.org/critical-controls.cfm As you organize your program, make sure your security architecture component includes an understanding of how well these controls are designed and operating for your critical systems.

A critical engagement point for general security controls is in the system design phase. As new systems are proposed or significantly upgraded, general security controls should be baked into the analysis, including an understanding of where gaps may exist in the ability to incorporate them. You may never design or upgrade a system where all the general controls you desire are able to be implemented. The most important point is that IT and business teams have visibility into what key controls are available and which are not. You will need someone with the authority to do so to sign and approve a risk decision to delay or omit key controls you would normally require to accompany the system.

Consider the following:

- The expected flow of information through the system under development, including data inputs and connections to the system, transmission of data between system components, storage of information, access to databases and other types of storage, connections to other systems and applications, connections to application data from other systems, and security of information outputs;
- The full range of security controls (e.g., policies, methods, procedures, devices, or programmed mechanisms intended to protect the confidentiality, integrity, or availability of information) necessary to protect live data;
- Identification of specific security controls required by business processes supported by the system under development (e.g., encryption of sensitive data);
- Evaluation of how and where security controls are to be applied (e.g., by developing a security architecture for the system under development);
- Review of designs to ensure security controls are specified and are compliant with organizational security requirements; and
- Documentation of security controls that do not fully meet requirements.

Asset Management

Disciplined asset management is key to any IT risk and information security program. How can you manage risk and secure what you don't know exists? Physical assets are still responsible for many sensitive information breaches despite leading practices in full disk encryption and other physical controls. Ensuring where your critical assets are, what they store and process, and how they are protected against theft is a basic capability for any program. Equally important, but in a different way, is your inventory of software. Making sure you are licensed adequately and procuring complementary software is important to a well-run organization.

Note: A new revenue source for many software companies are software licensing audits. Software companies will hire a third party, often a big accounting firm, to conduct an audit of your software environment in search of under-licensed products. If you paid for 10,000 licenses, but have 12,000 instances running, the audit will reveal as much, and you will be asked to pay restitution to the company for the difference. The audits are self-funded because accounting and consulting firms that specialize in this almost always find untapped revenue on which they are paid a percentage.

Information about hardware/software should be recorded in inventories (e.g., asset registers) specifying a unique identifier for hardware/software in use, configuration, and its version and location. The accuracy of hardware/software inventories (or equivalent) can be achieved by protecting against unauthorized change, checking regularly against physical assets, keeping up-to-date records, and having periodic independent reviews.

A sound asset management program will have accurate inventories of both hardware and software, which makes for a defendable position to track these assets real time.

Backups

Backups of essential information (e.g., business information, systems information, and application information) and software should be performed frequently enough to meet business requirements, and with a defined backup/archive schedule or cycle that reflects the security classification and recovery time objective (RTO) of the information and software being backed up. Backup arrangements should enable software and information to be restored within the critical time scale (i.e., the time scale beyond which an outage is unacceptable to the organization).

There are many evolving technologies for backups and spinning/static storage prices continue to fall. Flash storage is gaining popularity and is a good option for rapid RTOs. Leading practice is to conduct layers of backups such that certain highly important information and systems can be recovered quickly while other data and systems can be backed up on more static, less expensive media. With the rise of ransomware attacking backups, it is important to understand your backup architecture so that adequate controls can be implemented to protect them. For example, at least one copy of sensitive information and systems should be backed up on a segmented network or a completely different destination to prevent an attack from moving east–west and infecting them. You should also encrypt backups so that this data at rest cannot be accessed without proper credentials.

Workstations and Servers

Workstations and servers are how work gets done in our modern workplace. If you have ever needed to go without your workstation or laptop for the day, remember how unproductive you felt? Given their important role in enabling our daily work lives, your program should spend adequate time and resources to protecting the valuable assets.

Workstations should be purchased from approved suppliers (i.e., those with a proven record of providing robust and resilient equipment), tested prior to use, supported by maintenance arrangements, provided with standard technical configurations (e.g., running a standard operating system, standard applications, and common communications software), and protected by a comprehensive set of system management tools (e.g., maintenance utilities, remote support, enterprise management tools, and backup software).

Workstations should be protected against unauthorized access by:

- Invoking time-out facilities that automatically log off workstations after a set period of inactivity;
- Applying access control mechanisms to restrict access to the workstation; and
- Using personal firewalls and encrypting sensitive information.

Malware protection software should be installed on workstations and configured to scan computer memory, executable files, removable computer storage media, e-mail, and downloads from the Internet. It should always be active, provide a notification when suspected malware is identified, quarantine files suspected to contain malware, remove the malware and any associated files, and ensure that important settings cannot be disabled or functionality minimized.

A server system is one that provides central processing capabilities such as a mainframe or a server. They should be configured in accordance with documented standards and procedures. There are several great resources available that provide security configuration baselines, depending on the operating systems of the server. Consider the following as fundamental:

- Disabling or restricting functions or services;
- Restricting access to powerful system utilities and server parameter settings;
- Using time-out facilities; and
- Performing key software updates (e.g., patches and security fixes).

Server systems should be protected against unauthorized access by disabling unnecessary or insecure user accounts (e.g., the guest account (or equivalent) for Windows and UNIX systems). Because of their importance to multiple users, you should consider changing important security-related parameters (e.g., passwords) to be different from the defaults set by suppliers and invoking time-out facilities that automatically log off workstations after a set period of inactivity. Access to powerful system utilities and server system parameter settings should be restricted to a limited number of trusted individuals and restricted to narrowly defined circumstances (e.g., for the duration of an authorized change).

Threat and Vulnerability Management

Managing threats and vulnerabilities in your environment will typically fall under the security operations team. Be clear with your boss, stakeholders, and workforce; threats are ever evolving and vulnerabilities can never be fully remediated. There should be a program in place that is continuously evaluating threats (they change over time) and identifying high-risk vulnerabilities that your resources need to focus on.

Here is an example: In the health care industry, the greatest threats were historically well-intentioned insiders who accidentally disclose protected patient information to unauthorized parties. While that remains a threat vector, many health care organizations have recently been attacked with ransomware, often delivered via phishing e-mails. This threat landscape has shifted dramatically for the health care sector and security professionals are now reacting to this reality. On the vulnerability side, any scanning tool run against an IP range can tell you where you have vulnerabilities and fill up a voluminous report with things to repair. The art form with vulnerability management is to scan and monitor your most critical assets (maybe the financial databases and servers) and identify the critical or high-risk findings needing remediation. If, and it's a big if, you remediate all critical and high-risk findings, you will have achieved tremendous success and can then move onto medium- and low-risk findings.

Another way to discover and plug vulnerabilities is to actively monitor security-related events. Information about important security-related events might include the event type such as failed log-in, system crash, deletion of user account, and event attributes (e.g., date, time, UserID, file name, and IP address). Security-related event logs should be analyzed regularly (e.g., using automated tools), and include the following:

- Processing of important security-related events (e.g., using techniques such as normalization, aggregation, and correlation)
- Interpreting important security-related events (e.g., identification of unusual activity)
- Responding to important security-related events (e.g., passing the relevant event log details to an information security incident management team).

Correlation rules—or rules that aggregate security events for action—are an effective means to identify and prioritize legitimate security events requiring action. Examples of correlation rules include things like VPN log-ins from out of the country, multiple log-in attempts to domain controllers from untrusted sources, and so on. You may hear the term "playbook" when referring to correlation rules. Often, they are used interchangeably, but there is a subtle difference. A correlation rule or set of rules defines when alerts will fire and begin to fill up your log aggregation or SIEM platform. A playbook is a defined set of actions based on the alerts that fired. As an example, if you have an out of country VPN log-in alert fire based on a correlation rule you have established, the playbook should outline what steps your security operations or MSSP team should take. In this specific case, you will want to understand who the user is, establish whether and why they are using their log-in from out of the country (maybe they are working while visiting relatives abroad), and if any actions that need to be taken to sever the connection.

Another key process in your threat and vulnerability management is patch management. A patch management process comprises the steps required to manage updates to computer equipment, business applications, operating systems/software, and network components to address potential vulnerabilities. The high-level approach to patch management should (a) specify the requirement to patch computer equipment, business applications, operating system/software, and network components; (b) outline the way the organization deals with patching (e.g., what is to be patched); (c) cover testing requirements (e.g., provision of a test environment); (d) define methods of patch distribution (e.g., automated deployment); and (e) be approved by the system owner(s). A continuous vulnerability monitoring program can assist in identifying when new vulnerabilities emerge or systems fall out of compliance with current patching expectations.

Note that you can never patch everything everywhere. Most organizations evaluate what patches are the most critical, including security patches, and line up an appropriate maintenance window to perform the patch work. If there is truly a critical patch that closes a high-risk vulnerability in your environment, ensure there is an escalation path or emergency patch process that can address it within 24 hours. Unpatched systems are still a leading cause of network and application exploitation because they are known by everyone and usually easy to take advantage of with little to no skill. As recently as May of 2017, the *WannaCry* ransomware virus took advantage of Microsoft Windows SMB vulnerabilities that were identified months earlier with a patch available in March 2017. Organizations and individuals that applied the requisite patch were immunized against this attack. It is surprising how many large, global organizations with talented IT and information security teams were impacted by this attack when patching is so basic.

As previously mentioned, malware protection software should be deployed on systems that are susceptible to malware, which might include: relevant servers (e.g., file and print servers, application servers, web servers, and database servers); messaging gateways (e.g., those that scan network traffic and electronic messages in real time); desktop computers; laptop computers (e.g., those used by remote workers); and handheld computing devices (e.g., smartphones and tablets). There have been many security startups in recent years offering advanced malware protection to their customers. While I both endorse and have used these next-generation technologies, I would caution to overlapping capabilities and creating shelf ware. Back to the basics—defense-in-depth—protect the perimeter, protect the network, protect your applications, and protect your databases. In my opinion, it is better to have protections across all layers than to have all protections at one layer. The "onion model" is a useful way to explain to stakeholders where you are investing in resources and controls to combat attacks (Figure 3.8).

The onion model

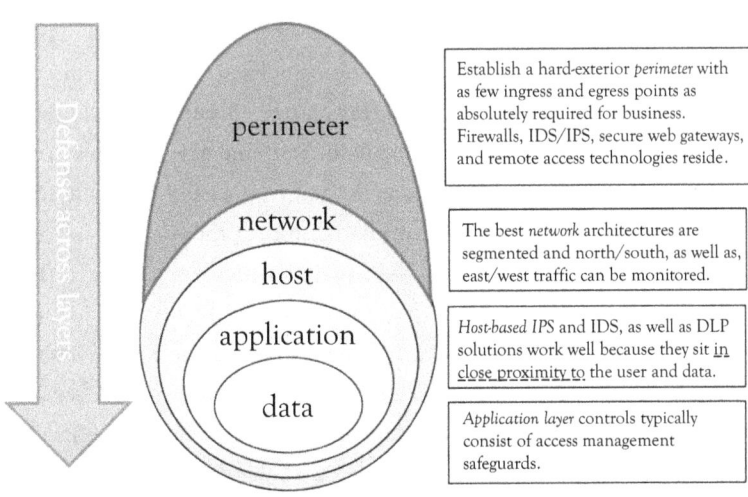

Figure 3.8 The onion model

A last bit on technology for discussion in this section are intrusion detection and prevention systems (IDS/IPS). A network intrusion detection system (NIDS) is a system that detects and alerts on attempted intrusions into a network where an intrusion is any unauthorized or unwanted activity on the network. A host intrusion detection system (HIDS) is a system that detects and alerts on attempted intrusions into a system where an intrusion is any unauthorized or unwanted activity on that system. Detection systems are reactive in nature and are often too late to the party to prevent a widespread attack. To address this issue, most technologies are moving toward prevention solutions. An IPS seeks to identify potential threats—in line—and execute a predefined policy thus preventing the malicious software from advancing to its destination.

Business continuity (BC) and disaster recovery (DR) capabilities are often the last consideration by security professionals. Sometimes these responsibilities fall within IT infrastructure teams or a specific group, depending on the size of your company. I would caution not to outsource this responsibility completely. Remember, security is about confidentiality, integrity, and availability. If your critical systems are unavailable, particularly because of a security incident, you will be asked what role you and your team had in preventing it.

BC/DR plans should contain a list of services to be recovered in order of priority; a schedule of key tasks to be completed, identifying responsibilities for each task (including delegates); procedures to be followed in completing key tasks and activities, including emergency, fallback, and resumption procedures; and sufficient detail so they can be followed by individuals who are generally unfamiliar with the process.

Perhaps most importantly, BC/DR plans should be tested regularly—using realistic simulations involving both users and IT staff—to demonstrate whether staff can recover critical information and systems within critical timescales. Contingency arrangements might include a separate processing facility ready for immediate use, reciprocal arrangements with another organization, or a contract with a specialty BC arrangements provider. Most CISOs choose to pay for a retainer of emergency response hours so that a SWAT team can be quickly assembled in the event the organization cannot recover on its own.

Like everything else discussed in this book, it is important to employ a risk-based approach in building your BC/DR program. There are several metrics used in the industry which can help you and your stakeholders determine what to prioritize and how to apply budget accordingly. One of the most important metrics is return to operations, or RTO. This metric, usually expressed in terms of hours, aligns you and your user community on how many hours of downtime can they live with in the event of an outage. Critical systems may have a four-hour RTO, while less critical systems may have 12 hours or longer expectations. Aligning on RTO is critical since the shorter the RTO, the more expensive it is to design the BC/DR program.

Regulatory Support and Policy Compliance

An information security policy outlines and communicates top management's direction on, and commitment to, information security. It defines information security, staff responsibilities regarding information security, and sets expectations on the desired information security behavior for individuals. Individuals with access to the organization's information and systems may include internal workforce, consultants, contractors, and employees of third parties (e.g., business partners, outsource providers, and vendors). Often policies are derived from regulations, standards, or leading practices that offer guidance on how information systems are to be used and protected.

Good polices are short (one to three pages) and are written in plain English. In my experience, it is better to have multiple, short policies on specific topics, rather than a 200-page comprehensive policy explaining everything under the sun. For example, have separate policies specific to remote users, acceptable use, and so on. That way, it is far easier to search, read, and reference. If more details are required to outline specific practices, consider creating procedures or guidelines that accompany the policy for those who need or require more information. Think about it from the nontechnical reader's perspective. Is it easier to search and reach a two-page policy or thumb through a 200-page policy for the section you need on page 186?

Legal and regulatory requirements impacting information security should be recognized by senior management, applicable business leaders, the head of information security (or equivalent), and stakeholders from other security-related functions (e.g., legal, compliance, operational/enterprise risk, internal audit, insurance, human resources, and physical security). A process should be established for ensuring compliance with relevant legal and regulatory requirements affecting information security. These include information security-specific legislation (e.g., computer crimes, electronic commerce, and encryption export), general legislation which has security implications (e.g., data privacy, investigatory powers, intellectual property, and human rights), and regulation (e.g., financial regulation, anti-money laundering, corporate governance, health care and other industry-specific regulations such as PCI DSS and HIPAA).

Depending on the industry in which you are operating, you could be highly regulated and spend a good deal of time making sure you have dotted your *i*'s and crossed your *t*'s. Be careful not to focus all of efforts on checking these boxes. Of course, you need to operate your department in a compliant and legal fashion, but I have always found if you do what is best for your organization, apply a risk-based approach to IT risk and security, you will always be on strong footing with regulators.

Skill Evaluations

A critical component of organizing your program is understanding the skills necessary to operate it. The adage of surrounding yourself with smart, talented people has never been more applicable than in the information security program operations space. At least twice in my career, as a security leader, I have been asked to evaluate the current staffing level and experience of the team I was hired to lead. This is your first opportunity to think and act like a business-minded CISO. It is always tempting to build an empire or ask for more staff than you think you may need, but this is a big mistake many nonbusiness-minded CISOs make.

The worst thing you can do is build an organizational chart based on perceived needs without having done a thoughtful analysis. I like to hire one person at a time and see how the work effort levels out over time. Understanding how many hours are needed to support operations and project work is absolutely required to determine the headcount and skills needed to be successful. When evaluating your team's skills, hold one-on-one interviews early in the process to fully understand, directly from them, what they do on a daily basis and also what they are interested in. You may find your staff are not being utilized optimally or you can get more from them if you put them in roles they are passionate about.

Even though information security programs require a technical workforce, the business-minded CISO also recognizes the value of business-minded security staff. Look for team members who can help you with the softer side of security—in addition to the data scientists, white hat hackers, and other technical resources you require. A well-rounded team and individuals are incredibly valuable to successfully operating your program, but also in evangelizing and selling your program's initiatives both within IT and across the business.

IT Risk Management Versus Security Operations Capabilities

As a business-minded CISO, you may have expanded responsibilities beyond information security. While information security risks are top of the list for most organizations, other risks such as business enablement (providing the IT functionality needed by the business to grow and prosper) and regular technology operations often create challenges for IT teams. Figure 3.9 gives an example of how some organizations divide IT risk management functions from security operations functions.

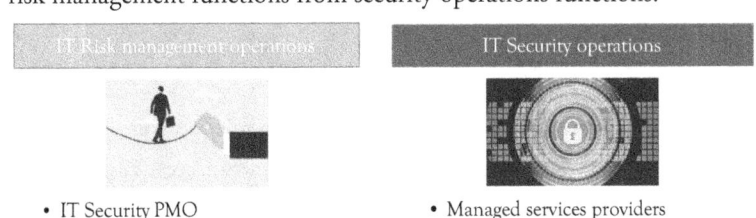

IT Risk management operations	IT Security operations
• IT Security PMO • IT Risk assessment / governance • Policy and standards development • Training and awareness • Audit / regulatory support • IT Vendor risk management • Management reporting – metrics	• Managed services providers • Threat and vulnerability management • Identity and access management • Data loss prevention (DLP) • Security incident and event monitoring (SIEM) • Security incident and event response

Figure 3.9 IT risk management versus IT security operations

Source: Risk icons from https://publicdomainpictures.net, Security icons from https://pixabay.com/

Of course, your organization may dictate other responsibilities, but these two broad functions cover most of what an IT risk management team would focus on. Back on skills assessments, as you determine which of these functions you will incorporate into your program, you should take the opportunity to organize your team by skills sets and align them to one or more of the functions under your purview. Cross training is a worthy pursuit for your team as often vacationing team members, unexpected departures, and other life events will create a scenario where a staff member who historically focuses on security operations may need to step in and assist with risk management. Well-rounded individuals obviously work out the best here.

Tip: Don't be afraid to publicize what your team does daily. Do it in the right way in the right forum, but let others know the breadth and depth of your team's activities so that they can appreciate how much you are accomplishing on behalf of the organization. This ongoing evangelization will help if budgets become tight or the IT department is asked to cut back overall. You will have already demonstrated and communicated your team's value proposition and therefore will likely be able to avoid financial and human resource reductions.

If you work at a very large organization, it is likely IT risk management and security operations are separate functions. If this is true of your organization, make sure that IT risk and security operations are closely aligned. The IT risk folks should be some of your best evangelists.

Build a Business Case: Develop Your Three-Year Plan

Here is the good stuff: In no other part of your role are you better able to convey your business-mindedness than when you are building your program business case and seeking financial and human resource support. Senior leaders in organizations are businesspeople. They see their world in terms of financial performance, growth, stockholder/board satisfaction, and other measurements not always aligned with IT risk and information security outcomes.

You have assessed your current program, designed enhancements along the people, process, and technology components, and completed your staff skills evaluations. You know what technology solutions you want to implement and what people and processes you need in place to make it happen. Now it's time to convince those who hold the purse strings. Again, this is the point of security leadership where success and failure are often decided. I have talked with many of my peers who get frustrated at the lack of support for their ideas and programs. When I ask what they are trying to do, it all seems reasonable; so, I tell them it must be the business case they are bringing forward.

There are two main reasons information security business cases fail:

1. They are written in technical jargon businesspeople don't understand and are not mapped to a return on investment (i.e., how does this enable the business?).
2. They present only one option.

Let's face it, this stuff should sell itself, but often it does not. You would think with weekly, almost daily news stories about hacking activity, ransomware, and denial of service attacks that the IT risk and information security teams would have a blank check ready to hand over to your program. That is unfortunately not the reality. You as the security leader are responsible for selling the business case and it must address the two typical failure points listed previously.

Technical Jargon and Return on Investment (ROI)

If your CEO, CFO, and sometimes CIO cannot understand what you are asking for and why, your chances of getting what you want will be significantly diminished. Explain your ideas using simple terminology as well as use analogies they may more easily understand. For example, instead of using the term "malware sandboxing," say something such as, "fake environments which mirror your real ones and trap suspected malicious software so it can be evaluated for legitimacy." While verbose, this will certainly be easier for the layperson to digest.

Additionally, ROI is a phrase business leaders understand, so utilize it to sell your program. As an example: "By implementing our fake environments ... we will be reducing the risk of actual malicious software reaching our workforce by 95 percent." That's compelling and reducing risk is about the best ROI you can provide to any company.

Providing Options

Raise your hand if you like the same dinner option every night. Exactly. Your senior business leaders will appreciate options too when they see your business case. I typically present two or three alternatives for senior executives. As the IT risk or security leader, you will likely not have full visibility into all the financial and human resource demands across the organization. Therefore, it is better for you to offer a set of low, medium, and high investment options and let them decide where their comfort level and risk appetite resides. Figure 3.10 is an example of a two-option business case slide. Note there is still a recommended investment level, but now senior management can look at the options, the impact on maturity and risk reduction, and determine which direction they would like to pursue.

It should also be stated that it is important to understand the difference between operating and capital expenses. Accounting may not be of interest to you, but sometimes how things can be paid for determines whether you will get funding. Recently, it seems capital is easier to come

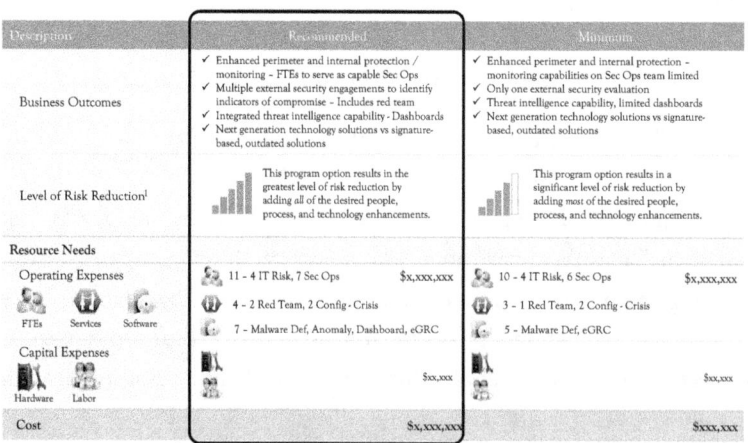

[1]Does not assume elimination of risk/exposure; other components, such as training and awareness, are critical for overall success.

Figure 3.10 Sample business case presentation

by than operating budget. Working with your vendors to produce quotes that can be capitalized can mean the difference in getting the technology solutions or not in years when operating expense is running short. Remarkably, I have in the past been given more than my recommended amount because excess budget in one business area was going unutilized and was not able to be rolled from one fiscal year to another—an obvious big win.

Summary Points

1. Organize your program the way you want but try to reference authoritative sources from which your key program functions were derived. You will achieve greater and faster support for your efforts if your stakeholders and colleagues have a common framework or reference model around which to rally.
2. Regardless of the exact names of your program functions, you should always apply safeguards/controls that address people, process, and technology shortcomings. Use a defense-in-depth model (or onion model) to organize and explain why and where you are applying these safeguards and controls.
3. The business-minded CISO is great at putting together business cases to justify investment. It's always best to provide multiple alternatives for your senior leaders to choose from so that they feel they have had an honest choice in how much risk they want to accept or how rapidly they want to mature the IT risk and information security program.

CHAPTER 4

Evangelize Your Program

Peer and Leadership Roadshows

The business-minded CISO recognizes the value in getting out from behind their desk and selling their program. In one position, the first time I visited with my organization's facility leadership forums and asked when the last time someone from IT came to speak with them. The entire audience responded with a resounding, "Never!" One of the first things I do when I take a new role is determine who my peers are—both inside and outside of IT—and what the major facilities and/or departments are with whom I need to build and maintain relationships.

Set up regular one-on-one meetings with your peers—monthly tends to work well for me. This will afford you the opportunity to get feedback from them on your program and its initiatives, as well as afford time for you to ask for their support and assistance when needed. If you have nothing of significance to discuss one month, there is nothing wrong with canceling the meeting and returning the gift of time. You will earn credibility with your peers by showing you value your relationship and you only want high-value time with them.

Leadership roadshows are your chance to reach a broader level of management within a specific department, facility, or unit. It can be difficult to reach every employee with your most critical messages, but line management is meeting with their staff regularly and you can leverage their reach into the organization to deliver key messages on your behalf. As an example, being extra vigilant about phishing e-mails is often an organizational focus. While I find sending monthly workforce communications about trending topics to be important, I find the time I have at management and leadership meetings particularly valuable because they enjoy being the bridge back to their teams. Once I even visited a few of my organization's big facilities and delivered their specific fake phishing campaign results as compared to the rest of the organization. In this instance, the facility I was visiting performed below average as it related to clicking on fake phishing e-mails (sent by my team) when compared to the rest of the organization. This facility's CEO and senior management team took it as a disappointment on one hand and a challenge to perform better on the other. This type of in-person relationship with the facility management team will undoubtedly assist in their performing better in the future and reducing risk to the organization. Is there any other reason needed to commit this time and effort?

I visit these management and leadership forums roughly once per quarter and present on various topics, typically for about 15 minutes. You don't want to wear out your welcome or dominate the management team meeting agendas so keep the content fresh, short, nontechnical, and take questions. I know I have been successful when I receive e-mails from the participants afterward with appreciations and follow-up questions. Make sure your presentation is high quality and tailored to their department or entity. When I go to speak with the Finance Department for example, I always have financial anecdotes ready to discuss. If you are at a clinical facility, make it real for clinicians. Remember, they think you sit in a dark cave somewhere and have no idea what they do on a daily basis.

External References

I always like to avoid the question, "Where did you come up with that?" When the business-minded CISO is out evangelizing his or her program, they should cite reputable sources for the reasons they are recommending certain courses of action. There is an alphabet soup of standards and frameworks (NIST, ISO, ITIL, etc.), research firms (Gartner, Forrester, etc.), and consultancies that you can tap into. Many organizations publish annual surveys that benchmark performance and provide industry insights and statistics. Where applicable, cite these sources to add credibility to your business case and ongoing initiatives.

In one CISO role I held, I was able to secure a 33 percent budget increase because I included an industry survey that benchmarked information security spend as a percentage of overall IT spend. It turns out that in my industry, most organizations were spending about 6 percent of their overall IT budget on information security. This may be a little on the high side for other industries, but the perception is that the health care industry is lagging and needs to spend more to catch up on deferred maintenance. At the time, my organization was spending less than 3 percent of the overall IT budget on information security, so by citing this statistic in my business case, I was able to convince senior leadership that a dramatic increase in budget was needed to catch up.

Don't be afraid to invite third parties in to evaluate and provide feedback on your program's progress. When I became CISO with one security department, it was a 1.72 out of 5.0 on the maturity model. After spending about 18 months implementing a three-year plan, I invited the same firm to return and refresh their assessment. I had just informed our governing body that I believed we had risen close to a 3.0 out of 5.0 since my arrival. The outside firm rated us a 3.2 out of 5.0, validating the progress we had made and further enhancing my credibility by accurately (and conservatively) self-assessing progress. In addition to progress validation, the outside firm provided updated recommendations to continue our maturity and risk reduction journey.

If you are confident in your program, you have nothing to lose by citing and using external references. In fact, if you shy away from it or begrudgingly share your plan with others, it says you may not be doing the right things and send a big red flag up to senior management.

Communication and Stakeholder Engagement

You cannot reach everyone in your organization through one-on-one and leadership meetings. You will need to establish a robust communication and stakeholder engagement process. Early on, identify your key stakeholders. They can be individuals, committees, teams, or whole departments in addition to the entire workforce. It is helpful to document these stakeholders in a spreadsheet or database so you can determine the frequency in which you communicate with them, discussion topics, and any feedback/action items you may have been provided. Figure 4.1 shows a simple example of how to organize your stakeholders.

Stakeholder	Frequency	Last meeting	Topics discussed	Feedback/Action items
Audit Committee	Quarterly	March 2017	Update on three-year plan, latest cyber threats	Asked next quarter to talk about the Internet filtering policy

Figure 4.1 Tracking stakeholder engagement

It takes extra effort and discipline to keep an up-to-date stakeholder engagement plan, but I have found it to be an invaluable tool for managing my interactions and delivering on my commitments.

Communications are an important facet of your program. You should categorize your stakeholders by segments of your workforce and tailor your communications for those specific audiences. Categories I have used include all workforce, clinicians, IT-only, and senior management. I typically send at least one communication to the entire workforce monthly. One month I might remind them about being diligent with regard to responding to phishing e-mails, but another month I will provide an update on emerging threats and other subjects of interest. I update senior management when there are significant accomplishments made in our program or there is a lot of public news about a cyber attack or threat. Giving the senior management team talking points as well as visibility into security efforts helps keep them engaged, connected, and knowledgeable. IT-only communications are typically produced when technical information or broad IT impacts to a security event are important to communicate. Clinician communications are tailored to their workplace and created in a nontechnical matter that is easily digested. Clinicians are very busy serving patient needs and don't have time to read detailed communications. I always make these communications short, easy to understand, and most importantly, informative about what they can do to protect against cyber threats.

A communications program can take many forms. E-mail is easy, and if your organization has a template you can use, you can create a campaign that workforce members will begin to recognize. Posters and flyers are also effective means of communication. Our team creates quarterly flyers and posters focused on a theme. We print them and we provide them to facility managers to hang and display in employee break rooms, cafeterias, and other back-office spaces.

Tip: Brand your communications. Create a logo or icon for your program that workforce members will begin to recognize and identify as your program.

Intranet Presence

Every organization has an intranet presence where corporate information, news, and online resources are located for convenient access by the workforce. The business-minded CISO recognizes that this tool can be extremely effective in evangelizing the security program. If you don't have your own department set of pages, you should. Frequently the IT risk management/information security presence resides with the overall IT department section. That's fine, but make sure you put ample effort into your sections so that they are resources everyday employees will find interesting and want to visit regularly. Here are a few sections I always create and maintain with informative content:

- About Us: organizational chart and contact information for you and the team;
- Resources: polices, guidelines, standards, and so on;
- Training and Awareness: web-based trainings, posters, and other training material; and
- News: interesting articles and news about your industry and the IT risk and cyber landscape.

If you have the resources for a full-time training and awareness coordinator on your team (I always make a strong case for one), maintaining your intranet presence can be part of their responsibilities. At the end of every roadshow and the bottom of every communication we send out, we list the intranet web link to our site. I encourage everyone to visit our site and utilize the resources located there. If you are going to actively market your site, you must make sure it is worthy of those efforts. I have hired professional web designers as contractors to get my site and resources up to snuff. Make a quality product and folks will visit it without a lot of prodding.

To measure what parts of your site are getting the most visits, you can typically monitor click counts to different resources and determine where folks are visiting the most. For example, sites with little to no traffic should either be enhanced or removed and replaced with pages that will receive visitors. Intranet site visits are a key metric I report out on each month so further justify the time and effort the team puts forth.

Summary Points

1. Make sure you put in the effort to plan and execute on your plans to evangelize your program. The best program in the world, if unknown or misunderstood, will not be as successful as one that the entire organization has some level of understanding and awareness of.

2. Use every form of media at your disposal to communicate your critical messages and provide access to your resources. It takes a little time to get workforce members to recognize your e-mail blasts and to find and visit your intranet site. Don't be discouraged if the volume of readership or take up of resources is low early on. After about a year of sending monthly communications, I began to hear from people during live conversations that my security bulletins were the only IT messages they read. Bottom line: Make them interesting and easy to understand and they will be broadly consumed.

3. Get out there! I cannot stress this point enough. Don't sit behind your desk and delegate the evangelism of your program to more junior staff. You are the leader; your workforce and leadership team want you out there selling and building support for your important work.

CHAPTER 5

Operate Your Program

IT Risk Management Capabilities

Policies and Standards

Policies and standards may seem like boring, administrative functions but they are the backbone to your entire program. Your program operates based on the policies, procedures, and standards you have outlined for all facets of your workforce.

Members of your IT department should follow standards when it comes to change management, configurations, new builds, and implementations. You give them the expectations upfront and when the Internal Audit or anyone else comes to check on them, they will have had the answers to the test ahead of time. As mentioned in the design sections, policies, procedures, and standards are usually derived from legal or regulatory requirements, leading practices, and/or human resource expectations. You will likely own the information security policies, and as the owner/operator of these policies, have jurisdiction over their scope, content, visibility, and revision cycles.

Ensure your policies, procedures, and standards are clearly written and available to the applicable audiences. You may have an IT-only section of your policy library where you post your database standards and that is fine; however, one of the most common audit findings and weaknesses in operating an IT risk management/security program is that lack of knowledge around—or even existence of—the documents that should dictate daily operations. If they are not being referenced regularly, they are just there to check a box and you are really doing your workforce a disservice. It is leading practice to at least quickly review these important documents annually to ensure they remain relevant and applicable and then do a full revision cycle every two years. Use your governance committees as sounding boards for significant policy changes and ask that they provide redline updates when their input is required.

Risk Assessment and Risk Management

Operating your risk assessment and risk management program is not difficult if you have designed and socialized it properly.

Risk Assessment

Risk assessment operations generally fall into two categories: ad-hoc/ongoing and annual.

Ad-hoc/ongoing risk assessments are those that are conducted as part of your technology review process or are born out of ad-hoc requests by the user community to bring in a new technology. As an example, a business leader may have just returned from a conference and have seen a demonstration of the latest and greatest analytics platform. You would encourage them to utilize the ongoing risk assessment process (the technical review committee); but then she informs you that she has already purchased it and now just wants to know how much risk she has introduced into the organization. You are now conducting an ad-hoc assessment to determine what, if any, risks need to have mitigation plans developed.

Also, of note with this circumstance: Don't blow up at this business leader for coming to you after the purchase decision. While it is always ideal to be upstream in the procurement cycle, if you castigate your business partners for coming to you later in the process, they will stop coming altogether.

Use the ongoing/ad-hoc risk assessments to build relationships with business partners and educate them on the organization's standards so they can become a more informed IT purchaser. It is very important that these types of assessments have their results documented in your risk register, that mitigation plans are assigned owners, and they are followed up on periodically. The whole purpose of these types of risk assessments are to catch IT risk as close to real time as possible and to establish risk owners, risk acceptors, and risk mitigation activities. Figure 5.1 gives an example of a snapshot view of current critical and high risks as an output of your risk register.

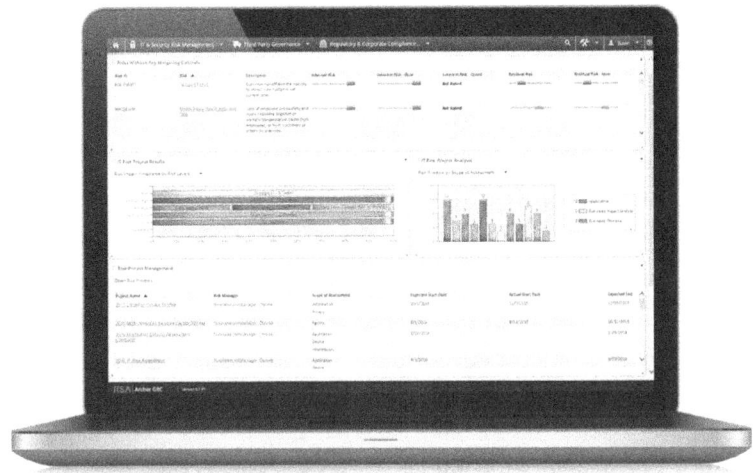

Figure 5.1 Sample risk register

Source: https://rsa.com/en-us/products/integrated-risk-management/t-and-security-risk-management

An *annual* risk assessment comprises the effort you put in during some part of the calendar year to talk with key stakeholders, review your current risk register, scan the industry for risk trends, and create a report that will serve as the basis for the following year's priorities. Many regulated organizations are familiar with these efforts and require applicable organizations to not only assess risk periodically, but also document the plans and activities in place to mitigate the identified risk.

These annual risk assessments can be time-consuming, so make sure you allot a few months out of the year to plan, execute, and report on them. For my annual risk assessments, I typically use a combination of online survey tools, in-person interviews, industry and consulting reports (trends), and the current list of risks documented in my risk register to serve as inputs. I also review any internal or external audit/assessment reports for parts that specifically identify the IT risk. After you have conducted your annual risk assessment, make sure you share your results (heat map example below) and tie your team's activities to mitigating these highest risk areas. I have always found it easier to secure budget and support for the IT risk management work if I can relate the project or initiative back to specific risk areas identified in the annual risk assessment report (Figure 5.2).

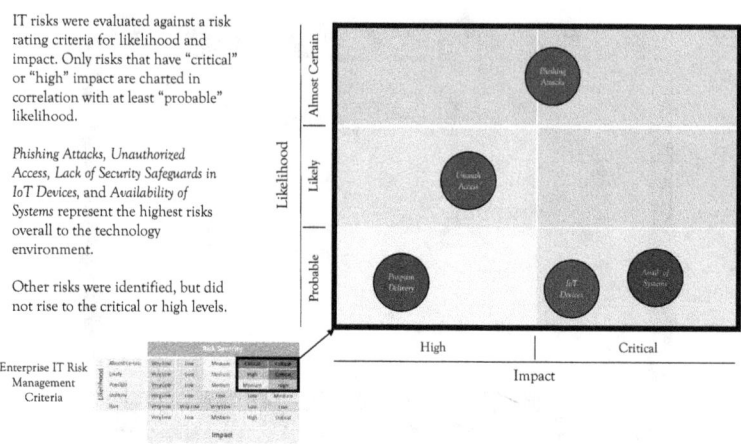

IT risks were evaluated against a risk rating criteria for likelihood and impact. Only risks that have "critical" or "high" impact are charted in correlation with at least "probable" likelihood.

Phishing Attacks, Unauthorized Access, Lack of Security Safeguards in IoT Devices, and *Availability of Systems* represent the highest risks overall to the technology environment.

Other risks were identified, but did not rise to the critical or high levels.

Figure 5.2 Example of an annual IT risk assessment heat map

With this heat map as an example of the organization's highest risks, management should expect to see initiatives in your program focus on preventing and detecting malicious attacks, unauthorized access, minimizing disruption of systems, and designing device security safeguards.

Risk Management

Risk management is not a complicated, theoretical practice. It is simply ensuring you have a way to identify risk in your organization (typically risk assessments), document your risk mitigation activities, and provide ongoing reports on risk mitigation progress. This is a cyclical process that requires both IT and business stakeholders to be bought into your risk management program.

When a risk is identified, an organization has the option to accept the risk (document it, but do not design any risk mitigation strategies), mitigate the risk (document it and apply risk mitigation strategies), transfer for the risk (document it, but have a third party or insurance policy mitigate the risk), or terminate the risk (decide to not move forward with the technology that is creating the risk). This process is referred to as "risk treatment." Which decision you choose is usually a function of how useful or how badly a system is wanted or needed. For example, if the technology proposed is going to cure cancer, but is not capable of having antivirus software applied, most would choose to accept or mitigate the risk. If the technology is for back office administrative personnel and will only have a few users but is not capable of having password protection, you might choose to terminate that risk by searching for another, more secure solution.

Risk management is the process of periodically reporting on identified and monitored risk. Seek out opportunities to report on what risks are open and active and what everyone in the organization is doing to mitigate risks with which you are living. The governance teams mentioned early in this book are excellent places to present these reports and provide transparency to senior leaders on what the IT risk landscape at your company is like at any given time.

Training and Awareness

Operating an effective training and awareness program is directly related to how invested you are in it. As mentioned in the design section, I have always found having a full-time employee dedicated to this is the best way to assure the requisite focus is there. This doesn't have to be a technical or even a security person, just someone who is outgoing, creative, and willing to put up with the technical members of your team wondering what their job is.

Once you have a needs assessment complete and campaign schedule established, operating your program just takes the investment of your time. With your training and the awareness thereby created, the employee should be able to create most of the content, print the posters, draft the communications, and so on. but the organization needs to see you—the IT risk and information security leader—out in front communicating the key messages. Have your FTE keep your intranet site and other resources up-to-date and fresh, while you get out to new employee orientation (NEO) (yes, you), IT department onboarding sessions, facility leadership and management meetings, and other training opportunities.

Provide oversight of your training and awareness program by treating each year's campaign as a set of projects. I have had a project manager assist my training and awareness leader with staying on track with quarterly content delivery milestones, monthly communication deadlines, and other facets of operating a disciplined and effective program. Measuring

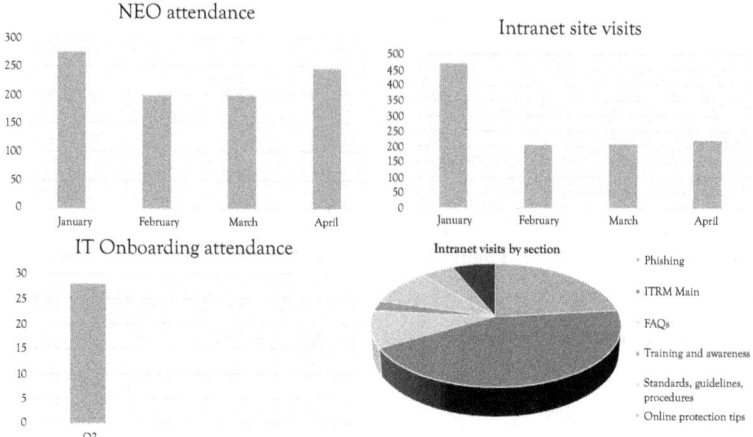

Figure 5.3 Example of training and awareness measurement

effectiveness in all areas of your program is important, including this part. Here is an example of a quick dashboard you can use to measure and report on your training and awareness effectiveness (Figure 5.3).

Be open to feedback on your intranet site and in-person presentations. Incorporate the input you receive to improve your survey results and drive more volume to your resources.

Project Advisory/Consulting

Project advisory/consulting efforts are closely linked to the ad-hoc/ongoing risk assessment activities described above but differ in the outcomes they provide. Your team should be very open to taking questions from, giving advice to, and providing general IT risk and security consulting services for the organization. This doesn't mean every phone call or e-mail is a risk assessment, it just means you are being a good partner and helping to manage risk in real time.

Make no mistake, having a project advisory/consulting function burns staff cycles and can be a distraction from normal operations and project work, but I firmly believe it is core function you must support. Here's how to make it less painful: If you have an on-call schedule, have the on-call staff member be the designated adviser for the day or week. That way, it rotates through your team (include yourself) and the burden of handling all the inquiries is shared. If you don't have an on-call structure, simply create a schedule that includes every team member (again, include yourself) that rotates daily or weekly.

Create a link on your intranet site titled *Contact Us* or *Have a Question?* That way you can have these questions or project advisory requests sent to a group e-mail inbox and the assigned staff member can tackle them via e-mail when they are free. Make sure you are timely in your responses. If someone leaves a voice-mail or sends a question via your intranet site, establish a reasonable SLA within your team, perhaps 24 hours that they will respond to the requestor. You may not have all the answers, but at least acknowledge the request and give the requestor a timeframe for a complete response. This practice will build credibility for your team and be a real value-add service your program provides.

Lastly, create a frequently asked questions (FAQ) section on your intranet site where you can document the most commonly asked questions or consultation outcomes. This practice will save you and your team massive amounts of time. Once a precedence has been established or a common practice adopted as the result of a consultation, you should strive to never have to answer that question again. Document the question, the answer, and the rationale so that if someone asks the same or similar question of your team, they can simply be directed to the FAQ site. Teach your workforce to fish!

Audit and Regulatory Support

Depending on the situation you walk into, this may be a mature function or need to be built from scratch. Assuming you worked that out in the *Organize* (Chapter 3) section of this book, it is time to operationalize it. In every one of my IT risk/CISO roles, the responsibility has fallen to me to help support our overall IT and regulatory efforts. Be careful—this expectation can take a lot of your time—and that is time not spent thinking strategically about preventing breaches.

To operationalize this function, I recommend either assigning an existing resource on your team or hire someone to specifically focus on this for you. The best people suited for this role are those with IT audit backgrounds and those who have perhaps worked in the public accounting space as an IT auditor or manager. At my most recent CISO position,

I did have this responsibility walking in. The audit and regulatory support function did not exist; therefore, I was expected to build it. One thing I learned quickly is that IT staff are not typically IT audit or regulatory savvy. If you put the right person or people in these roles you will be a big hit with your IT colleagues as they will quickly come to rely on your team to facilitate this work with internal and external audit teams.

Start with a partial FTE, if you can spare it, or hire someone to focus on it. Ultimately, in the scenario I inherited, I ended up hiring a manager level leader and three staff members to help support these efforts. It may sound like a lot, but the pressure from our internal and external auditors to get IT general controls and audit findings up to snuff created an urgency I tackled at once.

Here's a side benefit: While I regularly attend audit committee meetings to provide information security and IT risk updates, they are also keenly interested in the auditor's opinion of the control environment. Having this audit/regulatory support function within your department gives you an instant audience with the CFO, external audit firm, and the audit committee chair. Over the course of one year, the ability to put effective IT general controls in place elevated the information security department's stature and helped solidify the team's reputation for getting things done. Don't run from this opportunity; embrace it.

Management Reporting and Metrics

Now here is a hot topic. Whether you are trying to increase the maturity of your IT risk and information security program, or you just want to consistently communicate ROI to senior leadership, management reporting and metrics have become expected capabilities.

Don't try to measure too much or measure things that are too technical. The business-minded CISO should produce a one-page dashboard of meaningful metrics that can always withstand the, "So what?" question. There are good metrics and there are bad metrics.

Examples of good metrics include the following:

- Percent of workforce members who click on the last phishing campaign e-mail

- Percent of endpoints that have your newest DLP agent deployed
- Percent of managers who complied with your semiannual application access review campaign
- Quarter 2 program maturity score versus quarter one score.

Examples of bad metrics include the following:

- Number of attacks blocked
- Number of patches deployed last month.

Reporting and metrics that show relative change are the most valuable. Absolute numbers are worthless. If you tell your boss you blocked one billion attacks last month, does that really tell them how well you are doing? Sure, block one billion attacks but let three critical data disclosures leave the network. Good job!

Sarcasm aside, produce reports and metrics that are tailored to your audience. Your security operations team may want to track technical attack numbers and patching compliance, but your boss and the audit committee of the governing body will fall asleep during that report presentation. The dashboard below is an example of a board-level report that shows information security program maturity evolving from quarter to quarter and compares this program to industry peers.

This is the sort of information senior leaders and board-level executives want to see from you (Figure 5.4).

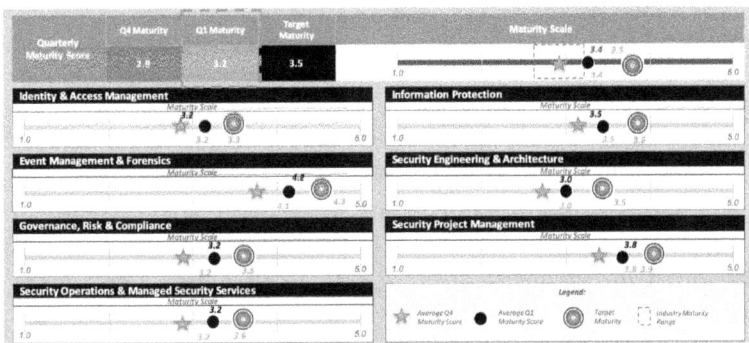

Figure 5.4 Example of a quarter-by-quarter program maturity measurement

Security Operations Capabilities

Vulnerability Management

Vulnerability management has, like many information security and IT risk functions, become commoditized. One only needs to look at how the pricing of vulnerability management tools has declined over the years to know that you can often afford multiple products if you want to have variety.

The skill associated with operationalizing this part of your program lies in what you are scanning (scope), how often you are scanning (frequency), and what you do about the thousands of findings you receive (prioritization). You can argue that by running a vulnerability management tool that you have operationalized it. That said, unless you are prioritizing the results by criticality, achieving coverage over the important parts of your environment, and assigning action plans with owners, you are just conducting a check-the-box exercise.

Here's what to do:

1. Define your critical IP ranges and segment them into scan windows.
2. Designate a routine day and time (after hours is usually better) where these ranges are routinely scanned—this will help create a normal behavior on your network so that other tools don't view the scanning activities as reconnaissance or attempt to attack.
3. Your tool should help you prioritize the most critical vulnerabilities (see Figure 5.5). Ensure those make it into your eGRC risk register and your security incident ticketing system so they can be actioned timely.
4. Designate at least one member of your threat and vulnerability management team to work these as they queue. That person should have relationships with network, operating system, and application team members so that they can quickly decide how best to remediate the findings.
5. The change advisory board or similar committee will be the body that reviews and approves remediations related to patches and upgrades. Make sure critical outputs from your scans make it to the committee.

Figure 5.5 Dashboard from a popular vulnerability scanner

Recognize and communicate with others that all vulnerabilities are not equal, and you may never get to the medium—and low-risk findings. It's no secret that anything released by a vendor as a critical security patch to address a vulnerability should be evaluated, tested, and deployed as quickly as possible.

Creating a process flow chart will help your team standardize the required steps to operationalize your vulnerability management program. It also helps train new staff and ensures consistency in business outcomes.

Figure 5.6 is a sample of a vulnerability management process flow:

Identity and Access Management (IAM)

Operating an IAM program can absorb the attention of one-third to one-half of your information security program personnel. It deserves that much focus because ensuring only appropriate workforce members, contractors, vendors, and affiliates access the minimum necessary and job-specific resources cannot be understated in maintaining a secure environment.

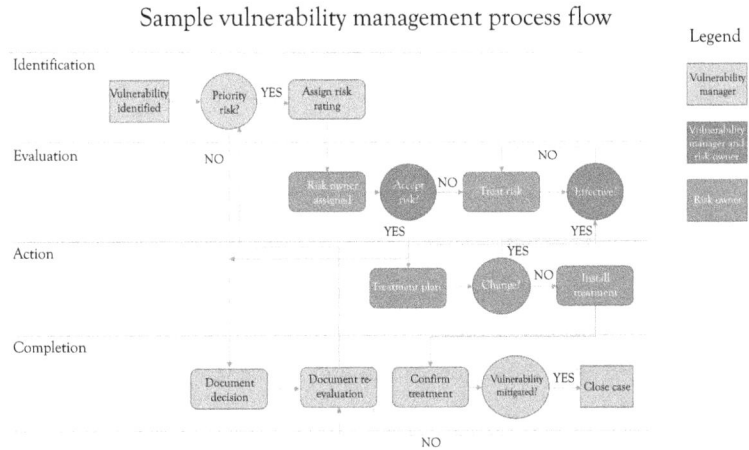

Figure 5.6 Example of a vulnerability management process flow chart

Do not forget about customers, patients, and others you will want to extend access to in order deliver your products and/or services.

IAM operations typically fall into the following processes:

1. Provisioning access
2. Modifying access
3. Terminating access
4. Reviewing access

These four processes apply to regular users, but also your privileged and special users who require more powerful access into your systems. Each of the four processes are described in detail below.

Provisioning Access

The process of provisioning access is typically the first experience an employee or other workforce member has with the information security department. Your team's ability to provision the right access, in a timely fashion, often dictates the reputation of the department early on. Most provisioning activities require tight coordination with the human resources department and human capital system.

One organization I joined had about a two-week lag between an employee's start date and their ability to obtain all the necessary system access they needed to do their job. That's two weeks of frustration, decreased productivity, and reputational damage directed at the IAM team. You do not want to be the leader of that group, nor do you want that to be the first thing your peers or senior leadership team thinks when they see you. Here's how to operate it correctly.

1. Understand the 90 percent of resources new hires need to be provisioned for on day one. Often referred to as birthright access, this access is required by everyone who joins the organization and does not vary based on job role or position. Once you inventory this list of basic access needs, work with your recruiting/human resources teams to get a list of new hires on a regular cadence and as early as possible. At a prior organization, we received feeds from human

resources about two weeks before a new employee starts, providing plenty of time to set up birthright access. Typical birthright access consists of:

- Network/active directory access
- E-mail and other office applications access
- Human resources, benefits, learning platform, and other administrative systems
- VPN access

2. Beyond birthright provisioning, you will always have groups of workforce members who need specific application access based on their job functions. In health care, that's usually physicians, nurses, and other clinical staff who need access to electronic charting systems, radiology systems, and so on. In other industries, similar situations exist where certain groups require additional application access support. Just as important as birthright access is understanding these groups and provisioning their access timely. I have had certain individuals assigned to provisioning clinical access specifically so that this important group of employees can be productive on day one. Imagine the frustration of a new nurse who shows up for their first shift at the hospital and cannot log in to the electronic health record system. You don't want that phone call.

3. Privileged or super user access always requires special attention and typically a special approval process. Generally, you don't need to worry about provisioning privileged access on day one, but because these employees are often database, system, or application administrators, you want to ensure extra levels of approval review and rapid provisioning for them so their important support functions can be carried out.

A final note on provisioning: Be certain you have a documented manager who is approving the provisioning of access. Every auditor on the planet will test your provisioning controls by looking at who has access to what and who approved it. You should try and avoid bulk provisioning processes (processes where one person approves multiple requests, usually with limited knowledge of the people for whom they are approving)

because they do not establish a credible approval hierarchy. Having a manager documented applies to contractors, consultants, vendors, and other
ancillary workforce members as well. In many cases, this is the riskier
access provisioning exercise. I have taken a stand and have stuck to it: *No
one gets access provisioned without an employee manager acting as approving
sponsor and being there to take responsibility for the access they want granted.*

Modifying Access

The process of modifying access usually gets the least amount of attention.
The problem with having loose modification practices is that long-stand-
ing employees often accumulate access resulting is a loss of the minimum
necessary principle and creating a situation where segregation of duties or
conflicts of interest can introduce risk.

In an ideal world, managers and human resources teams would be
proactive and inform your IAM staff when a workforce member changes
roles, but most of the time that does not happen. If a workforce member
needs additional access in their new role, you can bet you will be contacted
(use that opportunity to review all their access), but rarely will a manager
contact you and ask that you remove excessive access. Operationalizing
modification of access will be covered in the *Reviewing Access* section.

Terminating Access

Terminating, disabling, or removing access timely is one of the most
important functions of the IAM team. This is another area where auditors love to pull lists of active access in various systems and match them
up against active employee lists to determine whether access remained in
place after an employee left the organization. In addition to good security practice, you will want to establish—usually via policy—an acceptable duration of time to pass for your team to terminate access once an
employee terminates.

At one prior organization, we strove for access removal within 48
hours, which I believe is a best practice. We had some tools that removed
birthright access immediately, but that extra application access or special
access sometimes takes a little more effort and coordination to remove. As

with modifying access above, terminating access should happen timely, but the reviewing of access process can act as a "back stop" control to prevent terminated users from retaining access after they are gone.

Reviewing Access

Reviewing access is an important function to operationalize, and here is why: All the access processes described above are proactive attempts to provide, change, or remove access timely. If your team and workforce are mature in these functions, they may operate perfectly fine. If you are new at access management, often these attempts to manage access proactively fall short.

To operationalize access review activities, you should establish—again via policy—a frequency by which access is periodically reviewed by your management team. A strong suggestion is that birthright access and access to the highest-value applications are reviewed every six months. This semiannual review should ideally be managed by an identity governance tool; however, low-tech methods such as spreadsheets or e-mails could also be used if you do not have such a tool in place.

Caution: Do not attempt to review access for every application and system in your environment! Reviewing birthright access and access to your most important applications will mitigate most of the risk presented by lack of termination or modification processes. Additionally, the business-minded CISO knows managers have their regular jobs to do and access reviews for their staff are a distraction many resent. Send them access reviews for your most important systems only as no one will buy into reviewing 10,000 lines of access entitlements for their employees.

During your access review activities, do not overlook your contractors, vendors, and other nonemployees (Figure 5.7). The reason you need a manager assigned to these constituent groups is so you have someone to whom the access review will be sent. I call these access review processes "campaigns" and I would encourage you to do likewise. Because you will be asking front line managers and senior executives to act on your behalf, you should communicate the access review campaigns via e-mail, news flashes, town halls, and anywhere else you can get the word out. You are asking for their help in performing this important function, so make sure they know what to do, how to do it, and by when. Lastly, do not expect

First half year access review campaign

- Campaign ran from March 1th - April 15th
- 25 critical applications in scope for the campaign
- 186,542 accounts and entitlements were reviewed
- 3,825 accounts and entitlements were revoked
- 2,692 managers participated in the review
- 97.9% of managers complied with the access review

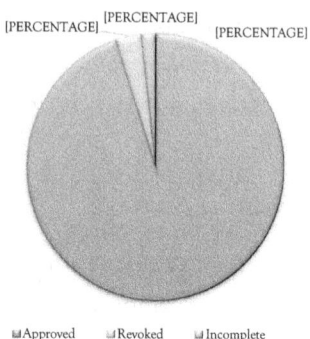

⊔ Approved   ⊔ Revoked   ⊔ Incomplete

Figure 5.7 Reporting out on access review progress

100 percent compliance with this process. I have historically needed to follow up with managers who missed the access review request e-mails and therefore had not performed their duty. Even with follow-ups, sometimes managers are on extended leave or simply don't read e-mail.

I would be very pleased with about a 98 percent compliance rate, and depending on the size of your organization, 100 percent may never be achievable. After your campaign, send a status update to senior leaders and use this as an update to your audit committee.

To get to 100 percent access review, you will have to disable or terminate access for those workforce members whose manager did not validate their access. Make sure you socialize this philosophy with your boss and communicate the action to all managers. After my team has attempted to contact the remaining noncompliant managers, we set a date by which we will disable their employees' access so we can say all access has been reviewed. If you inadvertently terminate or disable access for someone who needed it, re-enable the access once their manager affirms it, and use that activity as an educational opportunity with the manager. For example, "If you would have reviewed your employee's access as part of the campaign, this wouldn't have happened."

Value-Add Identity Management

All the processes described above can be accomplished with little to no automation or technology tools. That said, using an identity governance platform can really help streamline these access processes. Birthright access can be programmed into these tools to take feeds automatically from the HR system and create a virtually hands-off provisioning process. Similarly, feeds from the HR system can be routed into these tools and terminations be handled automatically as well. Identity governance platforms are expensive and sometimes take years to fully implement, but once in place and configured, they can add a lot of value.

Biometric or proximity card access, SSO, MFA, privileged account management (PAM), and other technologies can really help secure your environment further and in some cases, make life easier for your workforce. Seek out these opportunities to automate your team's efforts (IAM can be quite labor-intensive absent these tools) and look for ways to use information security as a business enabler.

As a business-minded CISO, I am constantly rounding at facilities to hear what IT issues they are encountering and what the information security team can try to do to help. Here's a quick story about one of those visits: I was rounding at a busy clinical facility soon after I started my new role as CISO and quickly learned our clinicians were not enabled with any sort of smart authentication. Clinician after clinician told me they spent hours each week logging in and out of systems as they moved from room to room and floor to floor. One clinician told me, "I couldn't believe when I started here that we didn't have badge tap single sign on." Honestly, I couldn't believe we didn't have it either. Just to gather some empirical evidence, I enlisted a reputable vendor in this space to conduct an analysis of how many minutes and hours per week busy clinicians were spending because they didn't have this capability. The vendor was happy to do it for free since it's how they help sell their technology solution. The results of the analysis confirmed the feedback I was hearing. Busy clinicians spend anywhere from two to three hours a week manually logging into and out systems. I quickly gathered my IAM team and we began formulating a phased implementation plan. A year later, the solution is 20 percent deployed across the organization and the feedback has been tremendous. This is value-add identity management.

Data Loss Prevention (DLP)

Operationalizing your data protection practice quickly is critical to the overall success of your program. In each CISO role I have held, data protection has been the first place I start to understand the risk of data breach or leakage. Looseness around data protection safeguards will land you in the headlines and seriously question your ability as a security leader.

Historically, DLP systems have been the risk mitigator for data loss, and they still are for the most part. That said, with cloud computing continuing to grow and the traditional means in which we exchange information expanding, you must think holistically in your approach to data protection. Here are a few areas to consider and operationalize quickly:

- Corporate e-mail
- Personal e-mail and cloud storage
- Corporate cloud computing
- Remote access

Locations where data protection controls are applied:

- On endpoint
- At rest
- In transit

Let's explore these focus areas and locations in more detail. First, where is your sensitive data? This is probably the first and best question you can ask your team when you arrive as the new CISO. Just like IT asset management, if you don't know where your sensitive data resides, how can you protect it? The first thing to do to operationalize data protection is to inventory your sensitive data sources. Typically, data is stored in a structured environment (e.g., in a database as part of an application) or an unstructured environment (e.g., file servers, desktops, etc.). Structured data is a little easier to deal with as they are typically known by application teams, have some sort of security already applied, and are managed by IT administrators. Unstructured data tends to be all over the place, hence the adjective. Unless you work at a very small company, you will need the assistance of a scanning tool to crawl the environment and identify where sensitive data resides. These are enlightening activities. I'm always amazed at what I find on publicly accessible file shares, SharePoint sites, and other

Key Statistics

- Total corporate servers: **6,800**
- Database servers: **1,300**
- Database servers without sensitive data: **480**
- Database servers with sensitive applications: **898**
- Database servers being actively monitored: **695**
- Database servers under review for validation: **243**
- Database server platform: **Oracle, Microsoft SQL**

Servers with Sensitive Data Databases

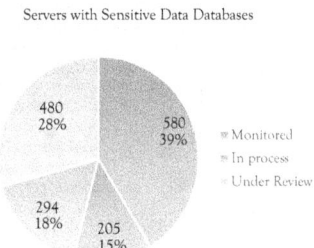

Figure 5.8 Example of a structured data report

collaboration media. You will want to design and implement safeguards that focus on these high-risk, typically unmanaged environments (Figures 5.8 and 5.9).

Once you have a handle on where sensitive data resides, you can begin to put the right technology solutions and processes in place to safeguard it. You should start in a place where data is transacted outside your corporate network. Usually that is the e-mail system.

Corporate E-mail

Corporate e-mail is a good first place to apply data protection solutions. Since e-mail is the most popular and expedient way to share information these days, it is also the fastest way to expose or mishandle information.

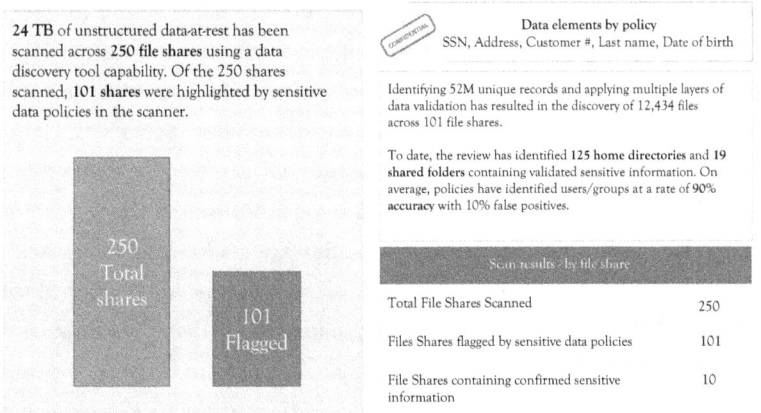

Figure 5.9 Example of an unstructured data report

Sharing e-mails between employees within the corporate network *is not* an area to spend a lot of time unless you work at the Department of Defense or some other highly restricted facility. In regular corporate environments, I don't know many security teams that encrypt data inside the network between the e-mail sender and the recipient. The overhead on the e-mail system and extra management required does not justify the small risk reduction you would achieve.

Corporate e-mail destined for outside of your network is a big risk area and should be tightly controlled with DLP and encryption solutions. These are mature technologies and places where some next-generation solutions are available to automate this work. On the DLP side, you should have a solution in place that applies certain policies based on your risk profile. Areas where I see consistent DLP rules applied are the following:

- Sensitive customer information (e.g., demographics, banking information, etc.)
- Intellectual property
- Privileged legal communications
- Electronic protected health information
- Credit card numbers

Most DLP systems allow you to customize the policies to filter on key words, numerical patterns, or other schema that you have deemed sensitive. They also allow for the setting of thresholds where different actions are taken based on the DLP rule and threshold achieved. Here is an example: All credit cards are 16-digit numerical patterns. You can tell your DLP system to alert on credit card numbers being sent externally from your network and then use your DLP system to block those e-mails from leaving, quarantine those e-mails and notify the sender, or allow them to go once the e-mail encryption system has encrypted them. You can set thresholds to manage risk along the way. You might block any e-mail leaving the network that contains greater than five credit card numbers, or you might quarantine e-mails that contain between two and four numbers, and you might allow one credit card number to leave if it is encrypted. These are all policy decisions; the technology solution will do whatever you tell it to in the rule sets, but the workflow and people impact will depend on how restrictive you set and enforce these policies.

The nice thing about data protection for corporate e-mail is that it is usually a highly managed system, has defined ingress and egress points, and there are many technical/automated systems that help with DLP and encryption.

Personal E-mail and Cloud Storage

Unlike corporate e-mail, personal e-mail and cloud storage sites are not managed by most corporate IT departments, have varying degrees of privacy and security reputations, and are as many as the day is long. These are risky egress points for sensitive data and ingress points for malicious software. The good news is that they all require an Internet connection to reach them, which provides you a choke point to apply security safeguards.

Some organizations take the safest approach—but least user-friendly—which is to block access to these sites from the corporate network. This is a quick configuration if you have a web proxy solution, a good firewall solution of a web isolation technology. Your administrators can simply block incoming and outgoing access to these personal e-mail and cloud storage sites. How do you know where your users are going? Cloud access security brokers (CASBs) are good solutions to understand the traffic to these sites and begin to lock them down.

Another approach, and one I typically employ, is to allow access to personal e-mail, but only once it is isolated using web isolation technology. I require personal e-mail and cloud storage solutions to traverse a cloud-based isolation platform that still allows workforce members to access their personal e-mail and cloud storage but does not allow uploads or downloads from them. This is the business-minded CISO approach. Blocking is easy; web isolation of these resources is a little more complicated, but workforce members really appreciate the ability to read and respond to personal e-mails and potentially read files they have in cloud storage locations. Another great benefit of this approach is that phishing e-mails, malicious attachments and links, and other bits of potentially harmful software are also isolated and do not reach your corporate network. If you haven't heard of this technology (it's relatively new), conduct an Internet search and you will find both generic and vendor-specific information about it.

In addition to web or browser isolation, network DLP solutions can typically enforce the same policies and rules on this web traffic as they would on corporate e-mail. If the DLP solution sees sensitive information attempting to leave the network to one of these cloud e-mail or storage solutions, the solution can act on it before it leaves.

Corporate Cloud Computing

Corporate cloud computing is here! Having worked in the IT and information security spaces for over 20 years, I can say with confidence that you can no longer deny it is happening. Cloud customer relationship management, HR, and other software as a service (SaaS) solutions are becoming more ubiquitous and even conservative corporations are seeing the value of "cloud-first" solutions. So, the sooner to accept that it is happening, the faster you can begin to partner with development and business teams to secure your environments.

I have often debated with other security practitioners as to whether they or these large billion-dollar cloud companies can better secure data. If your entire business model is to securely and efficiently provide data storage, computer, or development services, don't you have a better ability to fund and manage security solutions for it than we do? All the solutions previously mentioned—network DLP, CASB, web isolation—can help you secure your corporate cloud computing environment. More importantly, ask your cloud computing vendor(s) what they are doing to secure your environment. As part of any cloud services agreement, often the people and process parts of the arrangement are more important than the technical. Make sure you have their responsibilities and your responsibilities clearly articulated in the contract. For example, you may be responsible for access provisioning of your workforce to the cloud environment, but they manage the data protection aspects of data storage once it is in their environment. Also, make sure you have a cloud governance team. Many of the large breaches that have been in the news lately have resulted from initially secure cloud environments, but when changes or configurations to the environment were made, it exposed sensitive information to the public. Having a cloud governance team in place to review and approve changes to the environment will help protect your data.

Remote Access

Data protection processes and technologies typically apply rather easily to areas of your business where remote access is necessary. Whether via VPN, use of MFA, or other secure session and authentication mechanisms, data protection methodologies, like the ones described above, can be applied to the remote user. The important considerations with remote users and data protection is where are they, what device are they using, and what do you want them to be able to read versus download or save off the corporate network?

Like cloud computing, there continues to be a trend that companies can't avoid: A remote workforce. Whether they are contractors, vendors, or telecommuting employees, the ability to securely provision access to remote workers and control what information moves back and forth must be addressed. In operationalizing your data protection program, make sure you understand what your remote workforce user community looks like and what sort of data access they will need to do their jobs. In many cases, they may be connecting to a SaaS application from their home computer, essentially bypassing any on-premise or data center controls you have in place. This is where you will need to thoroughly understand the architecture of such arrangements and make sure your access, encryption, and isolation technologies are applied accordingly. As part of one cloud implementation, we as a business-mind information security department wanted to provide as much access as conveniently as possible to our remote users. We did that but did not allow files to be downloaded from that cloud environment onto anything except a corporate-managed device. You can view data and edit files in the cloud, but we specifically prevent those files from being downloaded onto a local, personal, unmanaged device.

On Endpoint

What is an endpoint? An endpoint device is an Internet-capable computer hardware device on a transmission control protocol/Internet protocol

(TCP/IP) network. The term can refer to desktop computers, laptops, smartphones, tablets, thin clients, printers, or other specialized hardware such point-of-service terminals and smart meters. (For help with other technical terms, https://whatis.techtarget.com/ is a great online resource.) In other words, pretty much anything can be an endpoint. Data protection on endpoint is the most effective place to enact safeguards because it is the closest proximity to the users. Here are a few tried-and-true endpoint protections as you operationalize:

- Full-disk/device encryption. Endpoints, because many are mobile, are susceptible to theft, being misplaced, or tampering. Most organizations protect the data that may be stored locally on endpoints by enabling full-disk or device encryption. If one of these endpoints is stolen, the data on the device is not easily accessible by the thief.

- Keep software up-to-date and do not allow local administrator accounts for end users. It goes without saying that data theft via malicious attack is most commonly the result of unpatched software being exploited. Keeping endpoint operating systems and application software patched will eliminate a lot of this risk. Similarly, do not allow local administrative access on endpoints. If the endpoint does become comprised, the first attack approach will be to utilize an administrative account to try and escalate privileges or gain access to sensitive information.

- Make sure DLP agents and browser isolation are deployed to endpoint devices. These are the devices most susceptible to poor user behavior or error. These technologies can protect users from themselves.

- Backups to allow for a restore if an infection cannot be eradicated. One of the most common ways to remediate an endpoint is just to reimage it, which means any data on the endpoint will be lost. Backing up data from endpoints to external drives or file shares will help ensure that data is protected and restorable if an attack devastates the endpoint.

- For true mobile devices (e.g., smartphones, tablets, etc.) use mobile application management (MAM) or mobile device management (MDM) technologies that can "containerize" sensitive information and applications.

At Rest

"At rest" is a strange term, but it's been around in security lingo for many years. At rest usually refers to data in data centers or in cloud-based databases. To protect data at rest, most security solutions revolve around encryption. I have two philosophies here based on real experience, not white papers or auditor feedback. First, encryption for many data center applications is difficult, adds a lot of overhead, and may prevent certain upstream and downstream systems from communicating with one another. I have never found it either feasible or worth the overhead to encrypt data at rest in data centers. In the data center environment, I typically rely on database anomaly detection tools and the physical access controls in place. If the data center is adequately secured physically and sound logical access controls are in place, the data should be able to be secured with DLP and in-transit encryption safeguards.

In the cloud environments we utilize I have a different, perhaps hypocritical philosophy. I ensure contracts with SaaS providers and hosting solutions have at least the same level of controls as my own security environment in place, but also try to negotiate they encrypt data at rest in my organization's cloud tenant. The reason for this different approach in the cloud is you surrender a certain amount of control and oversight when you enroll with one of these providers. I'm often confident in their security abilities, but because data may be comingled (and certainly comanaged) with other clients' data, I want extra levels of safeguards applied.

In Transit

In-transit data protection is the most obvious type of protection needed based on the ubiquitous nature of e-mail, FTPs, uploads to cloud storage and other Internet-based applications. Inventorying sensitive data source systems was discussed earlier in this section. Likewise, you should inventory the egress and ingress points to your corporate network. Do you know how many site-to-site VPN connections you have up and running? What contractors utilize your e-mail system? Do you have a corporate FTP server? Does it face the Internet?

Understanding how, why, and when data is in-transit in your environment will help you design and implement the necessary data protection safeguards. Most often, encrypted e-mail solutions, secure FTP sites, and others like transport layer security (TLS) will give you the protection you need to operationalize the in-transit part of your data protection program.

Security Incident and Event Monitoring (SIEM)

This is the good stuff. As with the operations of most security functions, it is easy to be lured into purchasing sexy software, dashboarding tools, and cutting-edge solutions. You may still want to have some of that, but sound and practiced processes (much more boring) are the way you operationalize and mature this capability at your company.

There are four main steps in the SIEM process:

1. Identification
2. Correlation
3. Triage
4. Containment

Identification

Identification of security incidents and events is key to knowing what is happening in your environment. In today's corporate environment, there are many security tools and technologies you likely have watching different IT resources. Without naming specific vendors, you should at least have the following types of technologies in place to identify potential security incidents:

- Endpoint antivirus or detection and response agents
- DLP (across endpoint, network, and e-mail systems)

- Identity governance and privileged account management systems
- Database and file anomaly detection systems
- Firewalls
- Web proxy and load balancer technologies
- Sandboxing/malware detection software

This is not an exhaustive list but represents a subset of what most mature organizations have put in place to identify potentially malicious or bad behavior. Each of these solutions, and others that you may have in place, should be configured to generate alerts based on events they are monitoring. Generating thousands of alerts (identifying potential incidents) is step one of a multistep process to keep your environment safe. Being able to sift through the false-positives and meaningful alerts you need to action takes place in step two, correlation.

Correlation

Correlation refers to the process of taking many inputs from the source systems described above and looking for places where one alert or log coupled with another alert or log adds significance to the incident or diminishes its importance. It's the process of corroborating what one alert or log is telling you by looking for evidence that another system is also alerting or logging abnormal behavior.

You will need an alert/log aggregation platform to efficiently manage the correlation activity at scale. It would be impossible to correlate the millions of events and alerts generated by these systems and log sources manually. Prioritizing what source systems from which you will gather alert and log information is vital to managing the volume of source data that is being processed by your correlation platform. You will quickly learn, based on licensing costs for these platforms, that you cannot log and correlate everything.

If you have limited aggregation capability, start by correlating these alerts/logs:

- Firewall alerts/logs

- Domain controller/active directory logs
- VPN/remote access alerts/logs

When you start adding all your server operating system logs and endpoint agent logs, the volume of correlation will skyrocket, so a process of continually evaluating what alerts or logs are adding value to the correlation process (and keeping them) and which are not a value add (and removing them) is critical.

MSSPs can help you operationalize at scale quickly. They will offer to put collectors in your environment that will ship as much data offsite to their correlation engine as you can afford. *Be careful. These can also become very costly. I have encountered many MSSPs that charge per log source and you, as the security program leader, are faced with a decision as to what to send them based on what you can afford.* I have opted to not put myself in that position and purchase my correlation/aggregation technology and host it on premise. I have found it to be more cost effective, if you have a large volume of data to correlate, to do it in-house.

Triage

To triage a security incident or event you first need to assess the severity of it and assign a priority to be investigated. Your security operations analysts should assess the severity of the alert received to determine whether an alert should escalate to the level of an IT incident.

Note that determination that an alert should be escalated can be subjective, and at the discretion of the analyst reviewing the alert. The probability that your organization will be unable to deliver services (availability) or will suffer a regulatory violation due to loss of sensitive data (confidentiality) should be considered high priority when assessing severity.

Examples of situations requiring escalation to an IT incident (not all inclusive):

- Evidence that an attacker has control of an organizational asset and is currently taking actions that could significantly impact your organization's confidentiality, integrity, or availability of systems and/or services

- A high-confidence alert indicating malicious activity inside your organization's network which might lead to destruction, disruption of services, or loss of data, for example, ransomware spreading through environment
- Evidence of exfiltration of your organization's sensitive data
- Situations not immediately identified as requiring escalation to an IT incident will proceed with Investigation activities. An IT incident may be called upon for collection of additional evidence.

Based on the assessment and prioritization of the incident, an incident response may be required. Based on the analyst's severity assessment, if it is determined that a security alert should be escalated to an incident, the analyst should notify appropriate management personnel and invoke the IT incident management process/playbook. Further investigation activities should proceed to confirm a compromise, including its breadth and depth.

Incident Event Response and Recovery

After triaging the incident/event, the next step is usually investigation of what occurred so to create a prioritized incident. When operationalizing incident event response and recovery activities, areas of focus are:

1. Investigation
2. Response
3. Recovery

Investigation

Gathering additional data is generally the first part of the investigative process. Your security operations analysts should gather any additional data necessary to ensure that a thorough assessment of the alert is completed. For example, if an IDS alert indicates that a system accessed a corporate resource, the analyst should check the system to determine whether the attack was successfully executed before requesting that the system be isolated, reimaged, or remediated in some other manner.

Often, there is not a single device or resource that has been infected or compromised. Your security operations analysts should enumerate other suspected infected hosts. Frequently, throughout the course of an investigation, an analyst may uncover indicators that will lead to other hosts not initially identified. These hosts should be cataloged as candidates also requiring some remediation action.

If a system is confirmed to have been compromised by some malware or malicious actor, accounts and/or sensitive information about the system should be gathered so further action may be taken. For example, accounts on a system found to be infected with a Trojan may need to have their passwords reset.

Finally, tuning of alert sources is a key step in completing the investigation process. False-positives are to be expected, even with the best correlation platforms around. In some cases, an alert source may need to be tuned so as not to continue to receive similar, unnecessary alerts.

Response

Based on the security analyst's severity assessment, and if further investigation determines the incident is substantiated, your security operations team should follow their playbook on containment and eradication. Following a standard set of procedures—including communicating with the IT help and others across IT—will help ensure your response practices are repeatable, timely, and effective.

The response may require coordination across facilities or geographies depending on the extent of the incident and number of IT resources impacted. In operationalizing your response processes, make sure you have identified team members who can help you respond quickly when an incident occurs. Having a security person or IT liaison that is familiar with the response process and ready to assist will greatly reduce the response time if travel or other logistical considerations should prevent your centralized security function from immediately reacting. Once the appropriate response has been followed through, your team and impacted users can begin recovery.

Recovery

The first step in recovering after an incident is to remediate the affected IT resource(s). Proper remediation steps should be followed for all convicted assets discovered through the investigation phase. Steps will vary depending on the supporting IT group and should be submitted in that group's preferred manner and tracked to successful completion. For example, a laptop recovery may just require a new image applied, something the desktop support team would likely handle. Whereas, if your human resources system was locked with ransomware, you may need to reload server operating systems and restore backup data to get back to normal.

Your security operations team should classify the incident and threat vector for key metrics and performance indicators to be developed. You might classify threats as such:

- Malware—bot
- Malware—virus
- Malware—Trojan
- Malware—rootkit
- Malware—worm
- Pup—adware
- Pup—spyware
- Reconnaissance scanning
- Web crawling
- False-positive

While this is not an all-inclusive list, it's a good place to start. You should also consider classifying your remediation actions. The appropriate remediation action should be classified for all convicted assets discovered during the investigation phase. Here are a few examples of remediation classifications:

- Requested reimage
- Sinkholed domain
- Sinkholed IP address
- No further action required

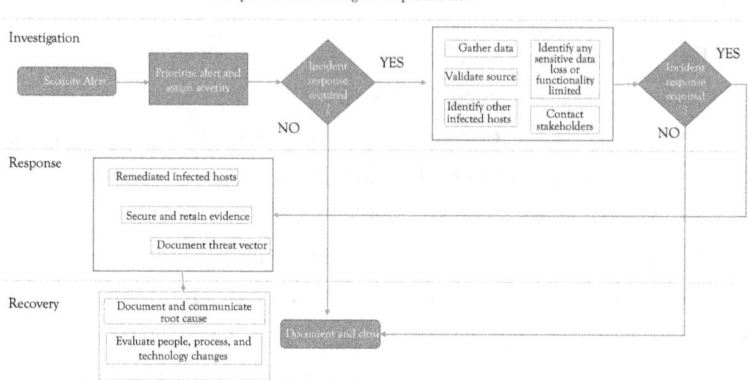

Sample incident management process flow

Figure 5.10 Example of an incident management process flow chart within an IT Risk Management (ITRM) function

- Blackholed host
- Account reset

Again, this is not an all-inclusive list, but rather some remediation classifications my security teams have applied in the past.

Lastly, you should be careful and diligent in maintaining evidence collected throughout the entire incident management and response process. Evidence of any actions taken by analysts should be maintained for audit and review purposes to the appropriate extent as deemed necessary within the appropriate standard operating procedure. If a public breach resulted from the incident, you can bet regulators, attorneys, and other outside parties will want to see everything your team did to identify, investigate, respond, and recover from the incident.

Flow charting your incident and event monitoring, response, and recovery processes will help formalize your operations and develop a repeatable, trainable process for your security operations team (Figure 5.10).

Summary Points

1. Operationalizing your program is much different from designing and evangelizing it. You will find that the people who help build your program may not be the right people to help you run your program.

Someone once told there are two kinds of people in the workplace—builders and operators. Be honest with yourself and with your team. Make sure you have the right mix of people to operate your program now that you have spent so much time building and selling it.

2. Consider managed services and a mix of onshore and offshore teams to operate your program. You may find that you don't have enough resources to support all the great technology and processes you have implemented. Similarly, you may have enough people, but they may not possess the requisite skillsets to operate and maintain your new program. Don't be afraid to shuffle your team around once you get into operations mode.

3. Look to emerging technologies and ways to automate your operations. A single bot built via a robotic process automation (RPA) effort can often replace the manual labor of multiple staff members. Bots work around the clock, don't make mistakes, and don't require benefits. That doesn't mean people are replaced; rather, repurpose them for more strategic efforts or projects you have forthcoming.

4. Last point: If you follow the guidance of this book, you will likely have a very successfully designed program, but your long-term success in operating it will depend on your ability to execute. Once your program is running like a well-oiled machine, turn your attention back to your leadership partners across IT and your key business stakeholders. Make sure the program is working for them too, not just you.

I wish you all the best! The information security industry has been very good to my family and I. Twenty years ago when I entered this career field, I had no idea this is where I would be today. Think creatively, think like a businessperson, be a business-minded chief information security officer, and success will follow.

About the Author

Bryan Kissinger is a seasoned IT and security professional with over 20 years of experience in designing and implementing practical IT risk and information security solutions that drive business value. Bryan is vice president of information security and chief information security officer at Trace3.

Prior to Trace3, he was the vice president and chief information security officer at a large integrated health system. He was responsible for the overall IT risk management and information security program. He was the leader of information and asset risk management strategies and security event and incident monitoring capabilities.

He is known for his ability to rapidly mature IT risk and information security programs and quickly deliver on the implementation of emerging technologies to solve complex business issues. He has served as the information security leader and or CISO at multiple large health care organizations.

Bryan also spent time consulting at Fortune 500 organizations across all industries in his role as a "Big 4" consulting practice leader. He is a Navy veteran and avid community volunteer.

Bryan holds a Bachelor of Science degree from the University of Maryland, College Park, an MBA from Chapman University, and a PhD in Information Technology Management from Capella University.

Index

OTHER TITLES IN THE BUSINESS LAW AND CORPORATE RISK MANAGEMENT COLLECTION

John Wood, Econautics Sustainability Institute, Editors

- *Preventing Litigation* by Nelson E. Brestoff and William H. Inmon
- *Buyer Beware* by Elvira Medici and Linda J. Spievack
- *Corporate Maturity and the "Authentic Company"* by David Jackman
- *Light on Peacemaking* by Thomas DiGrazia
- *Cybersecurity Law* by Shimon Brathwaite
- *Understanding Consumer Bankruptcy* by Scott B. Kuperberg

Announcing the Business Expert Press Digital Library

Concise e-books business students need for classroom and research

This book can also be purchased in an e-book collection by your library as

- a one-time purchase,
- that is owned forever,
- allows for simultaneous readers,
- has no restrictions on printing, and
- can be downloaded as PDFs from within the library community.

Our digital library collections are a great solution to beat the rising cost of textbooks. E-books can be loaded into their course management systems or onto students' e-book readers.
The **Business Expert Press** digital libraries are very affordable, with no obligation to buy in future years. For more information, please visit **www.businessexpertpress.com/librarians**. To set up a trial in the United States, please email **sales@businessexpertpress.com**.